Psalms of the Sisters

Psalms of the Early Buddhists

By

Caroline A. F. Rhys Davids

First published in 1909

Published by Left of Brain Books

ISBN 978-1-396-32618-9

First Edition

PUBLISHER'S PREFACE

About the Book

"The canonical tradition about the Psalms, and its historical significance, p. xiii. Reason for the prior appearance of the Sisters' Psalms, p. xiv. The Commentary and its functions, p. xv. The authorship of the Psalms, p. xvii. The legends of the Commentarial Chronicle, p. xviii. The Sisters in tradition's perspective, p. xviii. The Psalms as compiled aggregates of metrical memoirs, p. xix. The refrains, p. xx. The longer ballad or epic Psalms, p. xxi. II. The Psalms as expressions of the religious mind, p. xxiii.; and of its motives for leaving the world, p. xxiv; and of how the Quest, when found, was envisaged, p. xxv. Freedom, p. xxv. Mental development, p. xxvi. Consolation, p. xxvii. Arrest of the eternal round, p. xxix. Relation between teacher and disciple, p. xxxii. The new life, p. xxxiii. Analysis of the Goal, p. xxxvii. Inquiry into matriarchal survivals, p. xxxviii. III. Method pursued in translation and the metres, p. xxxix. Indebtedness acknowledged, p. xli."

(Quote from sacred-texts.com)

About the Author

Caroline Augusta Foley Rhys Davids (1857 - 1942)

"Caroline Augusta Foley Rhys Davids (1857–1942) was a Pāli language scholar and translator, and from 1923-1942 president of the Pali Text Society which was founded by her husband T.W. Rhys Davids whom she married in 1894."

(Quote from wikipedia.org)

CONTENTS

PUBLISHER'S PREFACE
INTRODUCTION 1
THE COMMENTATOR'S INTRODUCTION 32
PSALMS OF SINGLE VERSES 37
PSALMS OF TWO VERSES 48
PSALMS OF THREE VERSES 57
PSALMS OF FOUR VERSES 68
PSALMS OF FIVE VERSES 71
PSALMS OF SIX VERSES 95
PSALMS OF SEVEN VERSES 109
PSALM OF EIGHT VERSES 115
PSALM OF NINE VERSES 117
PSALM OF ELEVEN VERSES 120
PSALM OF TWELVE VERSES 124
PSALM OF SIXTEEN VERSES 129
PSALMS OF ABOUT TWENTY VERSES 132
PSALM OF ABOUT THIRTY VERSES 157
PSALM OF OVER FORTY VERSES 165
PSALM OF THE GREAT CHAPTER 172
APPENDIX 185
NOTES 195
ENDNOTES 197

INTRODUCTION

I

BOOK titles are necessarily brief. In their brevity they seem to claim too much and to specify not enough. Here and now let the title of this little volume be modified by the ampler designation: Verses attributed, in the tradition of the Pali Canon, to certain eminent Sisters (Therī-Bhikkhunīs) of the Buddhist Order, and forming the second and smaller portion of the work entitled Thera-therī-gāthā–i.e. verses of the Elders, Brethren and Sisters.

No one, not even, I imagine, a pious Buddhist, believes that these verses contain the ipsissima verba of those members of the Order to whom they are ascribed, or that these notable adherents conversed in Pali ślokas. We shall never get at the quantum of historic fact that there may be in the tradition, nor even know how many of the Elders here named ever really existed. Nor does it very much matter. The historical fact that we here have and hold is the record, that just the sentiments and the aspirations, which are expressed in this work, have been for so many centuries, and by a very considerable communion of followers, attributed to saintly men and women co-operating in the building up of certain ideals; and also that the logia should, as such, have been incorporated in a literature so long preserved, cherished, and revered as 'holy writ.' The registration of such views; the reverence accorded to such views; these are for the history of human ideas the really precious truths, however legendary or lost the genuine sources may have become.

The poems or verses so preserved to us are included in the Fifth Group of the second of the Three Pitakas (the Sutta-Pitaka) in the Pali Canon–the Group entitled Short: Khud'dăkă-Nikāya–and ranged after the Four Nikāyas often quoted in the following pages: Dīgha, Majjhima, Saŋyutt'a, Angutt'ără. The poems were edited with scholarly excellence in 1883 for the Pali Text Society,[1] then in the third year of its existence. Professor H. Oldenberg, now of Göttingen, was responsible for the verses of the Theras, or Elder Brethren. The late Professor R. Pischel, of Berlin, edited those of the Therīs, or Elder Women. The Brethren's Gāthās number 264, those of the Sisters, 73. Those of the Brethren come first. Bhikkhus formed the great majority in the Order, and, in standing and position, ranked senior to the Bhikkhunīs. The prior appearance of a translation of the latter part of the book is due, not to a wish to improve upon the ancient order, but to an accidental circumstance in the supply of materials. I refer to the Commentary on the Thera-therī-gāthā, and will turn aside to deal with it.

The gāthās, or stanzas, edited as above described, stand, as for nearly twenty centuries they have stood in the palm-leaf MSS. of the Sutta-Pitaka–that is to say, without any accompanying Commentary. In an Appendix, however, to his edition of the Therī-gāthā, Professor Pischel gave numerous extracts from Dhammapāla's Commentary on those verses. Ten years later this Commentary on the Therī-gāthā, together with its copious extracts from the Apadāna–the Vitæ Sanctorum of the Buddhist Canon–was published by the Pali Text Society in Professor Edward Müller's edition. [2]But, for some reason or other, the MSS. of the preceding portion of Dhammapāla's Commentary[3]– that on the Thera-gāthā–are not so numerous, or at least not so easily obtained as is the Commentary on the Sisters' verses, or the other parts of the work. At present I have heard of but one copy in Europe, now lent to the India Office on my behalf by the

Royal Library of Copenhagen, and that is neither a good nor a complete copy. My wants have now been better supplied by a copy purchased in Burma through the kind exertions of Professor Charles Duroiselle, of Rangoon College–a copy that he was able to procure without arranging for a special copy to be made at a Wihāra library. Had it not been for the lamentable deadlock of the long-promised Siamese printed edition of the Commentaries, a translation of the Brethren's verses might have preceded this volume.

This indeed has been the case in Dr. K. E. Neumann's vivid and vigorous, if at times somewhat free, translation of the Thera-therī-gāthā, into German verse. [4]He translated without the aid of any commentary on the Brothers' verses (a task bristling with difficulties), and with a 'thorough scepticism' as to the value of the commentarial chronicle about the Sisters. And in view of the shortness of life and the length of literatures, there is no doubt much to justify immediate translation of what we have, instead of waiting, to enrich and improve our work, for materials that we have not yet. To what extent such materials as I wait for do enrich and improve, the educated reader of past, present, and future translations must judge. If he is not acquainted with the tradition of the Buddhist Commentary, here it is in outline.

Whatever be the story of the Canon's evolution, while it had oral being only, it stands recorded that the Pali Canon was committed to writing in 80 B. C. Down to and after this date, the Attha-kathā, or 'talk about the contents, meaning, or purpose' of the work in question, was a matter of traditional convention, which individual expounding Bhikkhus or Bhikkhunīs might tell in more or less their own words. And when the Attha-kathā was about a Gāthā, the two together formed an Akkhāna (Sanskrit=Ākhyāna), a record or story in mixed prose and verse. The great work of the Jātaka or Birth-stories [5] is a notable instance of this.

About 80 B. C., then, the Psalms [6] were committed to writing. But in the fifth or sixth century A. D., either before or just after Buddhaghosa had flourished, and written his great commentaries on the prose works of the Vinaya and Sutta Pitakas, Dhammapāla of Kāñcipura (now Conjevaram, Madras Presidency), wrote down in Pali [7] the unwritten expository material constituting the then extant three Attha-katha's [8] on the Psalms, and incorporated it into his commentary on three other books of the Canon, naming the whole 'Paramattha-dīpanī,' or Elucidation of the Ultimate Meaning. He not only gives the ākhyāna in each Psalm, but adds a paraphrase, in the Pali of his day, of the more archaic idiom in which the gāthās were compiled, as well as the Apadāna citations alluded to above.[9]

All this, if read in a properly critical spirit, and with mindfulness of the effect of transmission and the long-time intervals on exegetists not versed in the canons of evidence and historical criticism, is of considerable help, both to the text editor, and to the translator, and to the reader. Professor Pischel has recorded, magnanimously modest, the help he derived from Dhammapāla, help of which his distinguished colleague and co-editor was, for nearly one-half of his editorial work, deprived for the reason already stated. To myself the Commentary has been indispensable. Without accepting in blind faith the accuracy of the synonyms or equipollent phrases supplied in its exegesis, I have, in many ambiguous terms, been determined by the ruling of the Commentator, as representing the most ancient orthodox tradition. Again, it will be seen that the gāthās often record different episodes in one and the same career, or the utterances of different persons whose identity has at times to be guessed at.

Now, the Commentator's explanations of episode and speaker are, it is true, legends woven out of legends. In the first place, of the seventy-one Sisters [10] to whom poems are attributed, we only meet with twenty in other works of the Pali Canon. The poems of half as many again are repeated in the Apadāna, but the names of the putative compilers do not always agree. A similar want of agreement between name and poem appears in the Saŋyutta version of certain of the Psalms given here in an Appendix. Hence it is only for a very limited section of the Psalms that we can, with any fraction of confidence, associate a given gāthā with a putative poetess for whom something approaching historical personality may be claimed. This does not, of course, warrant the conclusion that the majority of Sisters named as authors of gāthās, but of whom nothing is elsewhere recorded, never existed. But the fact that, in the Therī-gāthā and Saŋyutta Nikāya versions of certain gāthās, there is a discrepancy in five out of ten poems between poem and assigned author,[11] shows us that, if the verses were carefully preserved, the identity of the authors had, for the preservers, something of a Shakespearian or Homeric indefiniteness. And the fact, again, that in seventeen of the poems the Therīgāthā assigns one author's name, the Apadāna another, increases our want of confidence.

To this legendary status of the Therīs, as historical realities, we have to add the accumulated growth round their names of legend and myth revealed in the commentarial chronicle. For this growth Dhammapāla must not be held responsible. Its rate of progress had been much quicker. The canonical Apadāna, in its metrical tales of thirty-three of the Therīs, reveals their pre-natal legend already full grown. Besides, Dhammapāla drew his materials from three older Commentaries, as he himself admits. Now, even if we so stretch our less copious imagination as to concede to a few highly-gifted persons, just 'then' and 'there,' the supernormal power of visualizing that which they judged to be their own antecedent personalities in previous lives, there is no record whatever of Therīs, who claimed so to remember, recounting these reminiscences to their contemporaries. To this rule of reticence in divulging there are two marked exceptions. These are the last two poems, those of Isidāsī and Sumedhā, poems which, more than all the rest, suggest later literary craft, and, like the last few, bear the impress, not of traditional sayings handed down, but of deliberate literary creation.

Even apart from the, to us, mythological traditions attaching to each Sister, the record of her final rebirth does not always show signs that the scenes where she moved were, for the chronicler or for his authorities, choses vues. In one story we find the classic Gijjha-kūti, or Vulture's Peak, above Rājagaha, moved, apparently, to Sāvatthī. At Sāvatthī, too, is the Buddha found, while he is said to be preaching on the banks of the Nerañjarā in Magadha. And there are more such little 'faults,' geologically speaking.

But when all of that ilk is said and considered, the Western reader may still judge it well that the Psalms have been here presented along with, not in isolation from, their ancient if less venerable chronicle. All who are capable of a historical sympathy–of an appreciation, that is, of ideas as evolving in time–will be glad to see somewhat of the age-long traditions in which these rare and remarkable utterances have been set and fostered in so venerable a literature as that of the Pali manuscripts. Strangers to Christianity would have no conception of how profoundly the traditions grouped about the persons of the Virgin Mother and the Magdalene have permeated its history, who only knew the pale etchings of these women in the Gospels. Enshrined in the casket of legends constructed by the loving piety of centuries, these little poems of the Therīs take life and breath and colour. Whether the verses in search of an owner have perchance missed their way, whether, indeed, in some of the first few stanzas a name may not have been created to fit the words, still may we see, in this dream-pageant of Sisters of the antique world conjured up for us by the chronicler, the reiterated testimony to high quest, to devoted heart, to indomitable resolve.

The last-named feature, that of the Resolve and its persistent efficacy throughout rebirths, is of special interest. It is not characteristic of the earlier doctrine, but in Mahāyānist Buddhism, we find it taken up and elaborated, from the Hīnayānism of the Nidānakathā, [12]and of our Commentator into the Praṇidhāna's, or aspirations of persistent effect, formed when, in any human being, the bodhicitta (or heart of intelligence) awakes and transforms him into a nascent Bodhisatva.

But leaving the Commentary and reverting to the gāthās, it is very possible–nay, probable–that in all but the poems of a single śloka, and in some of two or three ślokas, later work of compilation may have been wrought on brief runes landed down from the beginning as the utterances of contemporaries of the founders of Buddhism. Another important and ancient canonical work–the Sutta Nipāta–would appear to have been thus threaded together. [13]It is not, of course, claimed that the Sisters, or any other notable Buddhists, spoke, however briefly, in blank verse; but it is held that, in early literatures, spoken utterances are ever the earliest records to be put in metrical form. And the Pali of practically all the Therī-gāthā is of ancient type. Moreover, under social conditions such as prevailed where and when Buddhism took its rise, that is to say, where there was considerable intellectual activity, but where writing was not used to register its products, there would be a tendency to convert with little delay all utterances deemed worth memorializing into metrical form.

Some of these metrical memorial utterances appear as the common property of several Sisters.[14] Once composed, it is quite conceivable that certain Sisters may have made frequent use of them in teaching and preaching. They may thus have become more associated with the memoirs of those Sisters than with the tradition attaching to others, whether the Sisters in question actually composed them or not. And where two or more detached stanzas were handed down, thus linked to the memory and tradition of one name, some member or members of the Sangha–man or woman, or both–of literary gifts may have welded them together, more or less, when the Canon was being arranged and becoming a closed work. An excellent instance of such a collection of detached gāthās, where no organic welding has been attempted, is that of Uppalavaṇṇā (Ps. lxiv.). Here are four episodes grouped about a name that occurs more frequently in Pali romance than any other woman's name.[15] The Therī is held up by the Buddha, according to Saŋyutta Nikāya, ii. 236, linked with another Therī, Khemā (Ps. lii.), as the standard and limit of what a woman in holy orders ought to be. But in the Vinaya, a Bhikkhunī, Uppalavaṇṇā, is thrice quoted in a connection that reveals her twice as an instance of a woman attractive to the other sex, and once as a student of weak memory. Another name, too, that of Ummādantī (enchantress), is mixed up with her legend. Hence the great Therī of supernormal power is as difficult to identify as our own St. George, and it is not strange that her gāthā should be composite.

The gāthā of Kisāgotamī (Ps. lxiii.) is another interesting case of possibly later work of welding. Here the tragedy of Sister Paṭācārā's life, no mention of which is made in the brief poem bearing her name (Ps. xlvii.), is woven into the Psalm called after Kisā-gotamī. And the fine summary of woman's 'woeful lot' is preceded by another brief episode on kalyāṇamittatā, or friendship with the good and lovable (καλοκάγαθοί). It is very probable from inspection of the poem (and chronicle), that of two poems attributed to Paṭācārā, one recounting her sufferings, given in the Apadāna and quoted in the Commentary, has been lost, or merged with that of Kisā-gotamī. It is also probable that the latter, if it introduces a gāthā already existing alluding to Paṭācārā, is of later date than this gāthā.

When we come to the last seven poems we find, not larger congeries of fragmentary sayings, but only homogeneous structure. The type approaches that of the ballad [16] or the incipient drama, or is a consecutive symmetrical monologue (Ambapālī, lxvi.). None of the putative authors, save Ambapālī, is an historical personage. And her poem is a type-lyric, not a personal document. It may have been composed by anyone of poetic gifts, and concerning ageing beauty in the abstract. Here, then, there is no question of sparse verses welded together and collectively ascribed to an age-dimmed, but very possibly genuine, personage. Either the Sisters in question composed these longer effusions, or they did not. According to Pischel, [17]'we have reason to suppose that' the ballads of Cāpā and Sundarī (Ps. lxviii, lxix.) 'are very old compositions,' because 'they bear the stamp of the oldest Indian ākhyāna as described by Professor Oldenberg.'[18]

But in the case of the last two Psalms, there are features pointing to different and possibly later conditions attending their compilation. Isidāsī's poem, for one who comes to it steeped in the phraseology of the preceding Psalms, strikes a strangely varied, almost a discordant note. The scene is Patna, a city rising on the decline of the Kosalan and Magadhese capitals, let alone that of Kāsī (Benāres). The wretched girl's plea to join the Order of Bhikkhunīs might be that of a Jain, so Jainistic is her aspiration. [19]The name of her sponsor Bhikkhunī–Jinadattā–which does not occur elsewhere in the Canon, is possibly significant. In the opening stanzas the work of editorial hands, as if dealing with less familiar material, is frankly admitted by Dhammapāla. Sumedhā's aspirations, on the other hand, have the older orthodox ring, even though often clad in different phraseology. But her harangues, differing in their copious flow from the severe and reticent terseness of the majority of poems, are sermons preached from a Bible: 'Remember,' she cries, 'this parable and remember that!' [20] as if the Nikāyas had already crystallized into shape. And where, in either Psalm, is the all-pervading influence of 'the Master' as a living presence?

How far editors of the earlier and authors of the later poems were identical, we shall never know. The canonical books are all, with one exception, [21]of too early a date to be claimed by any one author. 'They were the result rather of communistic than of individual effort.' [22] There is sufficient variety of style in all the longer poems, even though some of these are more mutually alike than others, for more than one author. As to the authors' sex, the genuine artist in words can give expression, with sympathy and verisimilitude, to the heart of man or woman. There seems, for all that, no sufficient warrant for Dr. Neumann's assumption that the poems of the Sisters, let alone those of the Brothers, 'must have been shaped by . . . a man.' [23] Not often since the patriarchal age set in has woman succeeded in so breaking through her barriers as to set on lasting record the expression of herself and of things as they appeared to her. But to assume that, because this happened seldom, therefore, this collection of documents, though ascribed to her, [24]are necessarily not by her, is to carry over far the truth: 'He that hath, to him shall be given, and she that hath not, from her shall be taken even that which she hath!' I make no counter-assumption that gifted Therīs had a hand in the compilation of the Brothers' Psalms. I would only ask English readers to await the appearance of those, and note the interesting differences in idiom, sentiment and tone between them and the Sisters' Psalms. Even the 'common stock' of refrains is different, the only exceptions being that of

> kataŋ Buddhassa sāsanaŋ,
> tisso vijjā anuppattā,

and

> n'atthi 'dāni punabbhavo. [25]

II

However, it lies with future historians of the Pali Canon as a whole to deal with these baffling questions. By whomsoever compiled, the contents of the Psalms are profoundly and perennially interesting as expressions of the religious mind, universal and unconquerable; a mind which is so intensely alive, because, to quote R. L. Stevenson, 'it knows what it prefers, instead of humbly saying Amen! to what the world tells it it ought to prefer.' Even in the shorter gāthās we may eliminate the common stock of refrains, and yet discern, in each residuum, a distinctly and pathetically individual note, telling its own story of a supreme 'conjuncture' seized, of Nibbana (in its later Sanskrit form, Nirvāṇā) or Arahantship won.

More interesting, to the social historian, than the peace they hymned is the account of the various motives that drove women, when Buddhism had arisen, from the world to embrace the an-agāriyā or homeless life. These motives are as diverse as those revealed in the records of Christian monasticism. Across time and space a common humanity is manifest. In some cases it is the drawing power of the Dhamma, preached by the

Buddha, or by a senior disciple of either sex, which brings about the crisis. The mental upheaval or commotion (saŋvega) produced in the hearer is occasioned, not so much by a 'sense of sin,' as by the flash of insight into universal impermanence in all things human and divine, and by the prospect of being reborn, world without end, in the infinite chain of life, ever renewing itself in the resultants of its own acts.

In other cases it is the vis a tergo of goading circumstance that impels the woman to break out of the groove. Escape, deliverance, freedom from suffering mental, moral, domestic, social–from some situation that has become intolerable–is hymned in the verses and explained in the Commentary. The bereaved mother, the childless widow, are emancipated from grief and contumely; the Magdalen from remorse, the wife of raja or rich man from the satiety and emptiness of an idle life of luxury, the poor man's wife from care and drudgery, the young girl from the humiliation of being handed over to the suitor who bids highest, the thoughtful woman from the ban imposed upon her intellectual development by convention and tradition. It is a suggestive point that the percentage of Sisters' Psalms, in which the goal achieved is envisaged as Emancipation, Liberty won–about 23 per cent.–is considerably greater than the corresponding proportion in the Psalms by the Brethren (13 per cent.). In most cases, the male singer had had the disposal of his life in his own hands to a greater extent than was the case with each woman. I do not so misread the poems as to conclude that the liberty they hymned was merely a shaking off the trammels of the 'House-life.' As a novelist of to-day sagaciously puts it: 'Only the selfish and the useless are ever free.' [26] 'CITTAŊ vimucci me!'–it was the freed mind, the release from sense, superstition, craving, and the round of rebirth that made them break forth into singing. All other escape was but the anagārūpanissaya, [27]the indispensable conditions of the final release. Nevertheless, these little women of old were every whit as human as we, and I am convinced that the glory of saintship was for them, and at first–when they hymned it–no white light, but prismatic through the circumstances and temperament of each. Thus, those who had had most ado in breaking away from the world were most likely to sing:

> 'O free indeed! O gloriously free am I!'[28]

and to climb alone and sit on rocky peak, where the keener air smote on their brow and the world grew wide beneath, while they mused on this good thing that had come to them:

> 'So sit I here
> Upon the rock. And o'er my spirit sweeps
> The breath of LIBERTY!' [29]

To gain this free mobility, pace the deeper liberty, they, like their later Christian sisters, had laid down all social position, all domestic success; they had lost their world. But in exchange they had won the status of an individual in place of being adjuncts, however much admired, fostered, and sheltered they might, as such, have been. 'With shaven head, wrapt in their robe'–a dress indistinguishable, it would seem, from the swathing toga and swathed under-garments of the male religieux–the Sister was free to come and go, to dive alone into the depths of the wood, or climb aloft.

Moreover, to free mobility she could wed the other austere joy of being recognized, at least by her brother 'Arahants,' as a rational being, without reference to sex. As such she breathed the spiritual atmosphere, she shared the intellectual communion of that religious aristocracy called in the Pitakas, Ariyas, with whom she claimed that power of 'seeing all things as they really are' (i.e., have come to be, sabbaŋ yathābhūtaŋ disvā), which the Buddhist called being Awake (buddho).

'How should the woman's nature hinder Us–

us Ariyas?' says Somā:

'What can that signify to one in whom
Insight doth truly comprehend the Norm?
To one for whom the question doth arise:
Am I a woman in such matters, or
Am I a, man? or what not am I, then?–
To such an one is Māra fit to talk!'

It is true that the Bhikkhunīs were, technically, appointed juniors in perpetuity to the Bhikkhus. It is equally clear that, by intellectual and moral eminence, a Therī might claim equality with the highest of the fraternity. In the Psalms an instance occurs, in xxxvii., where Bhaddā associates herself in spiritual attainment with the great Kassapa, successor, as head of the Order, to the Founder himself.

Not less touching than the sacrifices made for their dual liberty by rebels of the hearth are the few brief utterances of women who saw the land of freedom, but who repressed their longing to 'go forth,' even for many years, so long as duties to those depending on them kept them at home. To these the late-won liberty comes more as a haven of rest, and the poem a welcome spoken to her by the Master himself:

'Happily rest, thou venerable dame,
Rest thee . . . knowing Nibbana's peace.' [30]

It is worthy of passing note that these hindrances are chronicled as having been duties owed to husband, parent, or master, but never to children. If the mother's need is so great that she wrenches herself away from her children, either it is recorded that the child is handed over to grandparents, or the fact of the sacrifice is merely stated:

> 'Home have I left, for I have left my world!
> Child have I left, and all my cherished herds.' [31]

Whatever the mother's feelings may have been in such cases–and there are but one or two of them occurring in the book–the custom of the sons continuing to live with their parents after marriage seems to have been so prevalent that the children would not have been left unmothered. In nearly every case of a matron leaving the world, either no children are mentioned, or they are provided for, or grown up, or Death is mothering them.

For if Freedom drew, not less did Sorrow drive.

> 'Woeful is woman's lot! hath He declared–
> Tamer and Driver of the hearts of men;'

and there are many erstwhile broken-hearted women who, in these verses, tell of how they had found consolation. One noteworthy point is that, not only is there not the faintest suggestion of suttee, there is no case even of the widow so greatly mourning the loss of her husband as one beloved that she seeks comfort at the Master's feet. Where her 'lord' [32]leaves her to enter the religious life, she follows in emulation, and enters it with the Bhikkhunīs; but if she be widowed, she mourns either her impoverished lot, or she is, as it happens, mourning for a child, or for kinsfolk, at the same time. It is 'Rachel weeping for her children because they are not' that constitutes, far more than does the bereaved daughter, sister, wife, or widow, as such, the type of Mulier Dolorosa–

'Cuius animam gementem
Contristantem et dolentem
  Pertransivit gladius'–

to whom life in the Order came chiefly as comfort and support in mortal anguish.

The 'Light of Asia' has familiarized the West with the episode, narrated in our Commentary, of Kisāgotamī–the Frail Gotamid[33]–who, cheating her distracted mind, sought medicine for the little child she bore about, dead, on her hip. The poem ascribed to her is one of the most striking of the series. Released from all her sorrows by insight gained through communion in the Order 'with noble souls,' and chiefly through the object-lesson given her by the noblest of them all, she strikes in her verses a broader note. Into the echoes of her own grief she weaves the chords of the sufferings of her sex, and more especially the terrible experiences of her great colleague the Sister Paṭācārā,[34] as if to illustrate the teaching of him who had comforted her, namely, that 'there hath no trouble overtaken you save such as is commen to men.'

The Gotamid's swift acceptance of this stoic consolation may call up in contrast how a Western poet, with insight into human nature, spurns such comfort for the wounded heart while its anguish is yet raw:

'And common was the commonplace,
And vacant chaff well meant for grain.
That loss is common would not make
  My own less bitter, rather more:
  Too common! Never morning wore
To evening, but some heart did break.'[35]

But it should not be forgotten that Kisāgotamī, distraught though she was, is represented as being, in her spiritual evolution, at the very threshold of the Dawn, far nearer to saintship than the young Tennyson, mourning his friend, claimed to be. It is because he 'saw the promise in her,' that the Master judged her ready for the test he administered.

This method of consolation receives two developments in the poems. The former is essentially the agnostic position, and is the theme of Paṭācārā's own poem of consolation: 'So great a mystery was the little life now gone, both as to its coming and its going, that it never was yours–your property–to have or to mourn over. The great laws of the universe are not worked by you. Be quiet–und füge dich.' Thus are many mothers said to have been effectually comforted. Again we may feel sceptical, even scornful; but are we sure we have gauged the workings of all human hearts and every touch to which they will respond? Moreover, again, these were mothers ripe for salvation.

The other development alluded to is peculiarly Indian: 'No trouble hath overtaken you, save such as hath already overtaken you many and many a time in the infinite number of your past spans of life. Why, then, fall ever back on these helpless tears that never have availed aught? Cut at the source whence all these myriad bereavements have come.'[36]

Now, apart from their interest as a contribution to the history of women under Monasticism, the most salient object-lesson given by East to West in these Psalms is just this characteristic perspective taken of what we call 'life.' We have heard it said here that life is a moment between two eternities. But, as a normal attitude of thought, we wipe out the first eternity, and retain the moment and the forward view. In the religious language of the Buddhists–to speak only of this phase of thought–the word life, jīvita, hardly occurs. That which we call life is for them but one anga, one segment or stage, in bhava, or being (becoming) Their religious psychology, in the post-Asokan period, adopted the term bhavanga to mean just that moment (one out of an infinite number of moments) between the eternities, considered more especially as conscious, or potentially conscious, life, much as our psychology has adopted the less indigenous word continuum. [37]And accordingly, when these weeping mothers are reminded that times without number have they stood wringing their hands for the lost burden of sweetness unspeakable–ay, even there, at Sāvatthī itself, even here, in that charnel-field, even for a girlie called Jīvā ('living,' 'Viva') too,–even for many Jīvās–why then, for them at least, whose spiritual growth was just about to show the ripened fruit, all the intolerable uniqueness of this last bereavement fell away. No more could they say, 'Behold and see if there be any sorrow like unto my sorrow.' . . . The little moment of their bhava and of the child's bhava became merged into the past eternity. And the one thing needful rose up: How to merge the future eternity into the moment:

> '. . . had better live no longer than one Day,
> So she behold, within That Day, That Path!'

Not without reason may the Western mind of to-morrow object that this attitude too much resembles the hopeless outlook of the slum-cottage mother of to-day. She will remark of her dozen Jīvās: 'Ah, well, you must have your lot!' and also, 'As I ought to know, having buried nine!' To-morrow, it may be, living under physical conditions less horrible than at present, and with some training of the understanding, she will rise up and regulate both her 'lot' and let the lot live to bury her. Yet will one child here and there be torn by death from her. And the uniqueness will be the more intolerable then–or will she have heard of Ubbirī?

Thus, anyway, did the Buddha and his elect Sisters seek to comfort Rachel, administering no celestial balm, but educing from the tottering, anguished soul its inner resources, its latent self-reliance, its cramped faculty of spiritual vision. The Christian Bhikkhunī exhorted her sisters to

> 'Patere nunc aspera.
> Nunc sis Crucis socia,'

because they could expect to be

> 'Regni consors postea.' [38]

The Indian sister was bidden: 'Come to thyself!' and confessed herself victor over pain and sorrow:

> 'In that I now can grasp and understand
> The base on which my miseries were built.' [39]

But she is never led to look forward to bliss in terms of time, positive or negative. If Death be conquered, it is not through the winning, in Arahantship, of eternal living, but because, when Death comes, his eternally recurring visitation ceases. It may be that in harping in highest exultation how they had won to, and touched, the Path Ambrosial–the Amataŋ Padaŋ[40]–Nibbana, they implied some state inconceivable to thought, inexpressible by language, while the one and the other are limited to concepts and terms of life; and yet a state which, while not in time or space, positively constitutes the sequel of the glorious and blissful days of this life's residuum. Nevertheless, their verses do not seem to betray anything that can be construed as a consciousness that hidden glories, more wonderful than the brief span of 'cool' and calm they now know as Arahants, are awaiting them. There is nothing pointing to an Avyākata–an unrevealed mystery–concerning which 'we would, and if we could,' sing something. It may be with them as with one who, after long toil and much peril, reaches home, and is content with that for the day, whatever life may yet give or ask for on the morrow. They have won up out of the Maelstrom of Saŋsāra, they have 'crossed over,' they have won to something ineffable, that now is, but is not to be described in terms of space or after-time; and resting, they sing. We will leave it at that.

In practically every case the breaking out of the groove of habit and convention was proximately caused by a personal influence–magnetic, inspiring, persuasive–that of a ransomed sister or brother, or of the greatest Brother of them all. But herein we note a sharp contrast between these Indian Marys and their Christian sisters. Where He, the Central Figure, intervenes, and gratitude is blent with adoration, the little poem reveals no word of quasi-amorous self-surrender to the person or image of the Belovèd, such as characterizes not a little of that Christian literature for which the Song of Solomon–'I am my beloved's and my beloved is mine'–was a sacred archetype. The 'rex virgineus, sponsus dulcissimus,' who, in Abbess Herrad's psalm, 'prepares the bridal' and 'receives in his embrace,' belongs to a tradition naturally evolving around a youthful Saviour. [41]The utmost length a Therī presumes to go in relating herself to her Teacher, is to claim spiritual fatherhood in Him, whom she perhaps first saw late in his long life (some of the Theras, the Brethren, use the same language). Thus Sundarī:

> 'Thou art Buddha! thou art Master! and thine,
> Thy daughter am I, issue of thy mouth.'[42]

and, again, Uttamā:

> 'Buddha's daughter I,

Born of his mouth, his blessed word, I stand!'

And Uppalavaṇṇā:

'Thou who presumest to lie in wait for a child of the Buddha.'[43]

While for Kisāgotamī, her great physician enters her Psalm regarded, though not directly so addressed, more as a kind and noble friend (kalyāna-mitta).

In this connection, it should be noted, that, in Buddhist hagiology, there is no premium placed on the state of virginity as such. The Founder himself was a husband and father, and the most eminent Sisters were, three-fourths of them, matrons, not virgins.[44]

It is also worthy of passing remark, that of the four notorious Magdalens who found peace and purity in the Order of Bhikkhunīs–Aḍḍhakāsī, Vimalā, Abhaya's Mother, and Ambapālī–not one expresses any deep feeling of personal attachment to the Teacher. Had they been of such a temperament, it is probable their past life might have proved impossible for them.[45]

Not a less interesting circumstance is it, when the rescued soul's devotion fastens itself upon a woman saviour, as is shown notably in the loyalty professed for Paṭācārā, the Great Pajāpatī, Dhammadinnā and Uppalavaṇṇā. [46]The last two have individual acknowledgments paid them, but the first-named–a veritable Mater Consolatrix–is hailed by a school of Bhikkhunīs as their sovereign Lady

'Like unto Sakka o'er the Thrice Ten Gods.'

Hers is the system or sāsana that they obey; the Master himself is not for them in the foreground of their cult.

From whatever motive and through whatever agency the Sisters had found their way into the Order, it is clear that with the change a new and varied life opened up for them. We see in the verses the expression of energies and emotions newly awakened or diverted into new channels. Even where the poems breathe rest and peace, their tone is exalted and hedonistic, telling of

'exceeding store
Of joy and an impassioned quietude.'[47]

Even in the verses of those women who have sought refuge in the Order from overwhelming misery or disgust, there is little or no expression of the obtained relief in terms of that quiescence and apathy and mortified vitality so readily imputed to the religious ideals of the East. Life under the Vinaya was one of both active and contemplative discipline. The emancipation won implied 'space'–okāsa–opportunity, that is, for developing, regulating, and concentrating both thought and deed:

'La douce liberté cherchant la douce loi.'[48]

Under its régime the Bhikkhunī became the pupil of some Therī. She led the simple life, and discharged the ministering duties of a novice. And by prescribed exercises and daily lessons she worked out for herself, if the promise was in her, her own salvation, qualifying to become a teacher and leader in her turn. There was to be no forgetting by her of what she had left and escaped from. Not only was she to turn and mark those past struggles, but, as her insight grew, there was to come to her, if she was of the calibre of these Therīs, memories of former lives, revealing the inevitable working of the law of Kamma (karma), or the conservation of the effect of action. The vision might have its terrors, but it was all part of her Peace–for had she not made an end[49]–an end which all her days meant:

'. . . peace on earth.
Not peace that grows by Lethe, scentless flower,
There in white languors to decline and cease;
But peace whose names are also Rapture, Power,
Clear sight and Love: for these are parts of Peace.'[50]

Such are a few of the salient features in these little cameos of thought, carved by, or for, these notable women of long ago. It would take too long here to analyze, not only the motives that brought them into the Order, but the various aspects, peace and the rest, under which they viewed that adept state called 'Arahatta,' which they all are affirmed to have won, and the assurance of which is termed AÑÑĀ (lit., ad-sciens). I will only touch on one avenue opened up for the adept woman, that has ever been sought by her in whatever communion she graduated. For all her inspired musings under the hilly skies or the cool shade, the Therī's life was not wholly one of introspective reverie, free or regulated. The Order, refuge though it proved, was primarily an organization for the propaganda of the Dhamma or 'Norm,'[51] and its members were all, more or less, wholly or at times, saviours and good shepherds of stray sheep. Instances of this one and that 'teaching the Dhamma' will be met with in the Psalms and their story, notably those of Paṭācārā, of Puṇṇikā the serf, of Vāsitthi, and of Sukkā, pupil of the greater preacher, Dhammadinnā. Indeed, we find it not hard to picture Sukkā[52] pacing to and fro on the rostrum of her terrace, her audience sitting cross-legged or otherwise, enchanted, spellbound in the dappled shade around her, while from out of the venerable, once sacred tree, near which the group of cells clustered, the elfin face of the Dryad–her ancient votive shrine neglected, yet herself stirred to enthusiasm by this New Woman's eloquence–leans out from the trunk,

> 'fain to quaff
> That life's elixir, once gained never lost,
> That welleth ever up in her sweet words,
> E'en as the wayfarer welcomes the rain.'

Another Psalmist, Bhaddā Kāpilānī, is also spoken of in the Vinaya (Vin., iv. 290, 292) as a learned and honoured preacher of the Dhamma. And in the Anguttara Nikāya we meet with another Sister, called 'The Kajangalan'– namely, of that town–who, though no Psalmist, expounds to an inquiring congregation the very theme, the first question concerning which baffled her notable colleague, Bhaddā Curlyhair (Ang. Nik., v. 54 f.; Ps. xlvi).

The two instances–possibly versions of one and the same legend–of itinerant women debaters,[53] betray the breaking out of active intellects into less cramped, if unprofitable channels. Organized educational work in the Order must have proved greatly welcome to such temperaments.

It may assist readers to gain a purview of how the Therīs envisaged their summum bonum, if I give a summary of my own analysis, together with the number of Psalms in which each aspect is emphasized. The table is not exhaustive, and might be supplemented, and in most cases more than one aspect appears in one and the same poem. The End of Living or of Rebirths, e.g., forms almost a ground-wave to be discerned in the majority of the Psalms, if not always the surface-billow.

SALVATION, NIBBANA, OR ARAHANTSHIP VIEWED UNDER–

A. A NEGATIVE ASPECT.
(As a release, a getting rid of.)[54]

(a)	Nibbana (the 'going-out' of greed, ill-will, and dulness)	5 (vi., xlvii., lxiii., lxx., lxxiii.).
(b)	Freedom	17 (ii., iv., xi., xii., xvii., xxi., xxiv., xl., xliii., xlv.-xlvii., lii., lxiii., lxix., lxx., lxxiii.).
(c)	Comfort, End to Ill	11 (xxxiii., xlix., l., li., lv., lix., lx., lxiii., lxviii., lxii.).
(d)	End of Becoming or 'Life'	9 (xx., xxii., xxv., xxxi., xlii., xlv., lv., lxix., lxx.).
(e)	End of Craving	10 (xxv.-xxviii., xxix., xxxiv., lii., liv., lxii., lxxi.).
(f)	Rest	3 (i., xii., xvi.).

B. A POSITIVE ASPECT.
1. *Subjectively considered.*

(a)	Mental illumination conceived as–	
	(i.) Light	12 (iii., xxiii., xxx., xxxv., xxxvi., xlviii., lvii.-lxi., lxiv.).
	(ii.) Insight	8 (xxxvi., xxxviii., xli., xliv., liii., lx., lxiv., lxxi.).
(b)	State of Feeling:	
	(i.) Happiness	5 (vi., xxi., xxxix., lvii., lxxiii.).
	(ii.) Cool, calm, content ('sītibhāva,' 'nibbutā,' 'upasamo ')	12 (xiv.-xvi., xviii., xix., xxvi., xxxvii., xxxix., xli., xliv., lvi., lxx.).

	(iii.) Peace, safety	11 (vi., viii., ix., xxix., xxx., xxxviii., xlii., xliv., lvii., lxii., lxxiii.).
(c)	State of Will:	
	Self-mastery	14 (xv., xxviii.-xxx., xxxii., xxxvi., xl., xlv., xlvii., lvi., lvii., lix., lxi., lxiv.).

2. Objectively considered.

(a)	As Truth	3 (liii., lxiii., lxvi.).
(b)	As the Highest Good	1 (xlix.).
(c)	As a supreme opportunity	1 (v.).
(d)	As a regulated life	2 (iii., xlviii.).
(e)	As communion with the Best	6 (xxxviii., xlix., lxiii., lxvii., lxix., lxx.).
(f)	As bringing congenial work	5 (xxxiv., lxii., lxv., lxvii., lxxiii.).[55]

For those who are acquainted with the way in which, in Christianity, the cult of the Madonna and of women saints grafted itself upon, and in part sprang out of, the widely spread cult of tribal goddesses in Europe, [56]the question will arise: 'Can anything of the sort be traced regarding the veneration of these women's names in the Buddhist scriptures?' But we are not here dealing with a cult of a woman or women, hence we may scarcely expect anything of positive value to comparative research in this field. Very faint traits of affinity here and there may suggest themselves to the keen flair of the anthropologist. There is, for instance, the association between Therī and tree. Beneath some tree they are wont to sit, to stand, to preach. In the Appendix they are always said to be found beneath, not a tree, but a certain tree:–aññatarasmiŋ rukkhamūle. Again, while there is nothing in their names associating them with hill-shrines, as is the case with 'berg and 'burg names of German women-saints, that the Therīs are found, for no very apparent reason, seated on hill-tops, I have shown. Once more, is there perhaps in the three sisters of Nālaka in Magadha–Cālā, Upacālā, Sīsupacālā–some echo of those local triads of goddesses, or saints that are common in German lore, and which loom, dim with antiquity, in the Semnai or Venerable Goddesses of Greek worship, [57]and in the Trinity of the Norns or Fates? Almost, finally, am I tempted to see significance in the form of the refrain adopted by or for the ageing ex-courtezan's Psalm–that of Ambapālī–

> 'So and not otherwise runneth the rune, the word of the Soothsayer,'

i.e., literally, the Truth-speaker. [58]There is no mystic association attaching to the word saccavādī, where it occurs elsewhere, hence I lay no weight on this choice of a name for the Master. Nevertheless it is interesting to find these two ancient institutions, the hetaira of the community and the Wise Woman, with her monopoly of seeing things as they have been, are, or will be, combined in one and the same poem.

III

In conclusion, let it be said that, while the text of the Commentary containing the life-history of each Sister has been here and there abridged and condensed, the verses have been translated as faithfully as lay in my power consistently with the attempt to convey something of the poetic and religious feeling of the metrical original. To do this for a foreign idiom and an alien and ancient tradition, it was often necessary to expand each bead in some rosary of terms into a phrase. E.g., the end of verse 337:

vītarāgā.
'Who also have themselves from passion freed,
visaŋyuttā
Unyoked from bondage, loosened from the world,
katakiccā
Who have accomplished their appointed task,
anāsavā
And all that drugged their hearts have purged away.'

No attempt has been made to force English into the Pali rhythms. Of these the one that is used in nearly all the gāthās is the śloka. It is as prevalent in Buddhist metrical diction as is the iambic five-footed line in ours. The line just quoted may be recited to illustrate it:

˘ ˘ ˘ ˘ ˘ ˘ ˘ ˘ ˘ ˘

_ _ _ _ _ _ _ _ _ _ _ _

V ī t a r ā g ā v i s a ŋ y u t t ā || k a t a k i c c ā a n ā s a v ā .

Where the metre varies, I have indicated the variety so far as I was able.

One of the more interesting varieties is the poem of Ambapālī, in which this once famous Thaïs contemplates her wasted charms. The metre is approximately that which came, in later literature, to be known as the Rathoddhatā (or Chariot-borne) variant of the Trishṭubh:

˘ ˘ ˘ ˘ ˘ ˘
_ _ _ _ _

K ā ḷ a k ā b h a m a r a v a ṇ ṇ a s a d i s ā
J e t t y b l a c k l i k e - t h e - c o l o u r - o f - t h e b e e

˘ ˘ ˘ ˘ ˘
_ _ _ _ _ _
V e l l i t a g g ā m a m a m u d d h a j ā a h u ŋ.
T h e c u r l i n g t i p s o f t h e h e a d g r o w t h o f m e w e r e.

˘ ˘ ˘ ˘ ˘
_ _ _ _ _ _
T e j a r ā y a s ā n a v ā k a s a d i s ā
T h e y t h r o ' a g e a r e - l i k e - h e m p - a n d - b a r k:

˘ ˘ ˘ ˘ ˘
_ _ _ _ _ _
S a c c a v ā d i v a c a n a ŋ a n a ñ ñ a t h ā .
S o o t h s a y e r ' s w o r d n o t o t h e r w i s e.

But in two or three cases I have not been able to identify the metre. [59]Studies in Indian prosody so far have been made chiefly in much later literature, when verses were largely made for metres. In these early rhythms, the poet may have been less hampered by precedent and convention.

Where the English limps lamely (I pass over the lack in the translator of poetic gift or training), this is in part due to a desire to put in no religious tropes and figures from Western traditions. Where they have intruded, notice of the exotic element is given. Some day the Pali gāthās will find their William Morris, their Gilbert Murray. In this makeshift venture, I have striven to make the translation such that the English reader, mindful as he goes of wayside warnings in footnotes, might feel confident that the lines before him do not omit subject-matter that is in the original, nor add subject-matter that is not. [60]At the same time, let it be readily admitted that the renderings are so far free as to disqualify the book from serving as a 'crib' to the student. If my gifted German predecessor in this effort could not adhere literally to the text, the English language, with its abhorrence of compound words, its poverty in prefixes and verbal nouns, starts him who wields it at a yet greater distance from the Pali. To regulate the more careful reader's confidence, or want of it, in the renderings selected, many words in the Index will be found with the Pali originals appended.

One more word in this connection. If I have used 'Sister' in preference to 'nun,' it was not, in sooth, that the latter term, in its original connotation of nonna, or mother, was not an adequate, and more than adequate, rendering for Bhikkhunī. It was rather to keep my Indian recluses free from such implication of confinement within walls and to lifelong vows as may now attach to the word 'nun.'

It needs no confession of mine to place on record the help I found, at the initial stage of translation, in Dr. Neumann's translation of the gāthās, as well as in Professor Windisch's prose rendering of the verses in the Appendix. That with regard to the former, the differences in German and English metrical idiom, combined with, here and there, difference in judgment, should have often led me to reach the end by a different way, does not by any means obviate the fact of the aid received. Pioneers had been step-cutting before me, and all honour to pioneers.

> 'Ukkādhāro manussānaŋ
> Niccaŋ apacito mayā.' [61]

And as my husband, seventeen years ago, introduced me to these dear and revered ladies–

> 'So me dhammaŋ adesesi therīhi suppakāsitaŋ'

–so now has he furthered and guarded my efforts with advice and criticism.

Gladly and gratefully would I record the kindness of those who have helped me in procuring the illustrations–to wit, Mr. J. H. Marshall, Director-General of the Archaeology Survey of India, who sent me many photographs of Rajgir, Sahēṭh-Mahēṭh, and other places; Dr. T. Bloch, of the Indian Museum, Calcutta; Mr. C. H. Hooper, of Messrs. Thacker, Spink and Co., Calcutta, who sent me several forest scenes; my brother, C. W. Foley, of Calcutta, who procured for me a selection of views about Gayā; Mrs. Arthur Schuster, who laid her large collection of photographs, taken on her Indian travels, at my disposal; Mr. and Mrs. Ernest B. Havell; and lastly, Mr. F. J. Payne, hon. secretary of the Buddhist Society, G.B. and I., who has given me valuable assistance in carrying out the work of illustration. Through their prompt and generous aid the book might have been interleaved throughout with interesting views of the ancient haunts of the Sisters, had it been practicable.

C. A. F. RHYS DAVIDS.

ASHTON-ON-MERSEY,
July, 1909.

THE COMMENTATOR'S INTRODUCTION

Honour to that Exalted One, Arahant, Very Buddha!

NOW is the occasion come for commenting on the meaning of the psalms of the Sisters. The exposition of their several poems will be made easier and more intelligible, if I first relate the circumstances under which the Bhikkhunīs in the beginning came to leave the world and obtain admission into the Order. Of this, therefore, I will give an account in outline.

When the Lord of the world had combined the Eight Factors–humanity and the rest of Buddhahood–when, having made his great resolve at the feet of the Buddha Dīpankără,[62] and mastering equally all the Thirty Perfections, according to the prophecy of the Four-and-Twenty Buddha in succession concerning him, he had reached the climax in his progress towards wisdom, knowledge of the world and Buddhahood, then he took rebirth in the Realms of Bliss (Tusita). And there, when he had lived the span of life among the ten thousand gods of the Cosmic Circles, he thereupon assented to the request of those gods to be reborn as a man that he might become a Buddha, according to their words:

'The time is now at hand when Thou,
  Great Hero, shouldst as man be born.
Bearing both gods and men across,
  Do Thou reveal th' Ambrosial Way!'

So he made the Five Great Considerations, and then, in the house of King Suddhodana, of the princely clan of the Sākiyas, did he, mindful and self-possessed, enter a mother's womb; then, mindful and self-possessed, did he there ten months abide; then, mindful and self-possessed, did he thence emerge and come to birth in the Lumbinī Grove.

Reared by divers nurses, surrounded ever in luxury by a great retinue, he grew up in due course, dwelling in one of three mansions, amid divers bands of nautch-women, and enjoying honours like a god. Then, anguish being stirred in him at sight of an aged man, a diseased man, and a dead man, he, from the maturity of his insight, saw the danger in the life of the senses and the profit in renouncing it. Mounting his horse Kanthaka, and with Channa as his companion, at midnight, through the gate set open by spirits, he went forth on the Great Renunciation. During the remainder of that night he traversed three kingdoms, and, coming to the bank of the river Anomā, and taking the outward marks of an Arahant, brought to him by the Brahmā-god Ghaṭīkāra, he left the world. Thereupon, as though he were already an Elder with the eight requisites, [63]comely in appearance and of graceful deportment, he came in due course to Rājagaha, and there going round for alms, he ate his meal in the cave of Mount Paṇḍava. There the King of Magadha offered him his kingdom. But he, refusing it, went to Bhaggava's hermitage and learnt his system; thence to Āḷāra and Uddaka and learnt their systems. Finding all that inadequate, he proceeded to Uruvelā, and there for six years practised austerities. Then, discerning that this brought no penetration of the Ariyan Norm, he said, 'This is not the Path to Enlightenment,' and, taking solid food, he in a few days recovered strength. So, on full-moon day in the month of May, he ate the choice food given by Sujātā, [64]and, casting the golden dish upstream into the river, he, full of his resolve, 'To-day will I become a Buddha!' ascended at eventide the Bo-tree seat–his praises sung by Kāla, king of the Nāgas–and there, in a quakeless spot [65] facing the eastern world, seated him cross-legged and indomitable. There, fixing his will in four respects, he vanquished the power of Māra ere the sun went down. In the first watch of the night he recalled his former lives; in the middle watch he purified the eye celestial; in the last watch he sounded the depth of the knowledge of the Causal Law. And, grasping in direct and reverse order the formula of causal relation, he developed insight, and reached that perfect enlightenment reached by all Buddhas but shared by no one else. There then abiding seven days in the Fruition which has Nibbana as its object, and, in the same manner, abiding yet other seven days on the Bo-tree seat, he partook of sweet food beneath the Rājāyatana tree.[66] Then, again, seated beneath the Goatherds' Banyan, he reflected on the depth of the essence of the Norm. [67]And his mind was disinclined for effort till he was entreated by Great Brahmā; but then he gazed upon the world with the Buddha-Eye, and, seeing all the diverse range of faculties in all beings, he promised Great Brahmā that he would teach the Norm. Meditating, 'Where, now, shall I first teach the Norm?' he discerned that Āḷāra and Uddaka had passed away; but then he thought, 'Very helpful to me were the Five who were attending on me when I broke off from my ascetic struggles. What if I were first to preach to them?' So, in the full moon of July, he went from the Great Bo-tree toward Benāres. And when he had travelled eighteen leagues, he met halfway the recluse Upaka [68] and conversed with him; and so on to Isipatana, where he convinced the Five by means of the Discourse called Turning the Wheel of the Norm, [69]beginning:

> 'There are two extremes, O bhikkhus, which the man who has given up the world ought not to follow' . . .

thus giving them, beginning with Aññakondañña, together with eighteen myriads of Brahma-gods, a draught of Truth-ambrosia. Then on the first day of the next fortnight he established also Elder Bhaddaji in the path of the Stream-winners; on the second day, Elder Vappa; on the third day, Elder Mahānāma; on the fourth, Elder Assaji; and on the fifth day, by preaching the sermon of the Mark of No-Soul, he established them all in Arahantship. Thereafter he brought over many folk into the Ariyan fold [70] –to wit, the fifty-five youths led by Yasa, the thirty Bhaddavaggiyans in the Cotton-tree Grove, and the thousand former ascetics on the ridge of Gayā-Head. And when he had established eleven myriads, with Bimbisāra at their head, in the fruit of Entering the Stream (conversion), and one myriad in the Three Refuges, he accepted the gift of the Bamboo Grove, and there abode. Now, when Sāriputta and Moggallāna, brought into the First Path through Assaji, had taken leave of Sañjaya (their teacher), had joined the Buddha with their respective followings, and had realized the topmost Fruition, he set them, who had attained the perfection of discipleship, over all his disciples. Then, going at the entreaty of Elder Kāḷudāyi to Kapilavatthu, he subdued the proud stubbornness of his kinsmen by the Twin Miracle, [71]and establishing his father in the Path of No-Return, and Great Pajāpatī [72] in the Fruition of Entering the Stream, and causing the princes Nanda and Rāhula [73] to renounce the world, he went back to Rājagaha.

Now it came thereafter to pass, while the Master was staying at the Hall of the Gabled House near Vesālī, that King Suddhodhana attained Arahantship while under the white canopy, [74]and then passed away. Then in Great Pajāpatī arose the thought of renouncing the world. Then there came to her the wives of those five hundred young nobles who had renounced the world on hearing, on the bank of the Rohinī river, the 'Discourse concerning Strife and Dissension,' and they told her, saying: 'We will all renounce the world to follow the Master.' And they wished that she should lead them to him. Now Great Pajāpatī had once already asked the Master for admission to his Order, and had not won his consent; wherefore she now bade her hairdresser cut off her hair, and donning the yellow robes, she took all those Sākiya ladies with her to Vesālī, and there entreating Him of the Tenfold Power through Elder Ānanda, she gained his permission to leave the world and enter the Order by accepting the Eight Rules. [75]And the others, also, were all ordained at the same time.

This, in brief, is the story. What is here said has been handed down at greater length here and there in the Pali Canon.

Thus ordained, Great Pajāpatī came before the Master, and, saluting him, stood on one side. Then he taught her the Norm. She, taking up under him the system of exercise, attained to Arahantship. The other five hundred Bhikkhunīs attained it at the end of Nandaka's sermon.[76] Now the Order of Bhikkhunīs being thus well established, and multiplying in divers villages, towns, country districts, and royal residences, dames, daughters-in-law and maidens of the clans, hearing of the great enlightenment of the Buddha, of the very truth of the Norm, of the excellent practices of the Order, were mightily pleased with the system, and, dreading the round of rebirth, they sought permission of husband, parents, and kin, and taking the system to their bosom, renounced the world. So renouncing and living virtuously, they received instruction from the Master and the Elders, and with toil and effort soon realized Arahantship. And the psalms which they uttered from time to time, in bursts of enthusiasm and otherwise, were afterwards by the Recensionists included in the Rehearsal, and arranged together in eleven cantos. They are called the Verses of the Elder Women (Therīgāthā), and they are divided into cantos of single verses, two verses, and so on, as follows:

PSALMS OF SINGLE VERSES

I

Verse uttered by a certain Sister, a Bhikkhunī of Name Unknown.

Sleep softly, little Sturdy, take thy rest
At ease, wrapt in the robe thyself hast made.
Stilled are the passions that would rage within,
Withered as potherbs in the oven dried. (1)

How was she reborn?

Long ago, a certain daughter of one of the clans became a fervent believer in the teaching of the Buddha Koṇāgamana, [77]and entertained him hospitably. She had an arbour made with boughs, a draped ceiling, and a sanded floor, and did him honour with flowers and perfumes. And all her life doing meritorious acts, she was reborn among the gods, and then again among men when Kassapa was Buddha, under whom she renounced the world. Reborn again in heaven till this Buddha-dispensation, she was finally born in a great nobleman's family at Vesālī. From the sturdy build of her body they called her Sturdykin. She became the devoted wife of a young noble. When the Master came to Vesālī, she was convinced by his teaching, and became a lay-disciple. Anon, hearing the Great Pajāpatī the Elder preaching the Doctrine, the wish arose in her to leave the world, and she told this to her husband. He would not consent; so she went on performing her duties, reflecting on the sweetness of the doctrine, and living devoted to insight. Then, one day in the kitchen, while the curry was cooking, a mighty flame of fire shot up, and burnt all the food with much crackling. She, watching it, made it a basis for rapt meditation on the utter impermanence of all things. Thereby she was established in the Fruition of the Path of No-Return. Thenceforth she wore no more jewels and ornaments. When her husband asked her the reason, she told him how incapable she felt of living a domestic life. So he brought her, as Visākha brought Dhammadinnā,[78] with a large following, to Great Pajāpatī the Gotamid, and said: 'Let the reverend Sisters give her ordination.' And Pajāpatī did so, and showed her the Master; and the Master, emphasizing, as was his custom, the visible basis whereby she had attained, spoke the verse above.

Now, when she had attained Arahantship, the Sister repeated that verse in her exultation, wherefore this verse became her verse.

II
Verse wherewith the Exalted One frequently exhorted Muttā while a Student.

Get free, Liberta, [79]free e'en as the Moon
From out the Dragon's jaws [80] sails clear on high.
Wipe off the debts that hinder thee, [81]and so,
With heart at liberty, break thou thy fast. (2)

This is the verse of a student named Muttā. She, too, being one who had made a resolve under former Buddhas, went on heaping up good of age-enduring efficacy in this and that state of becoming. Finally, she was reborn in this Buddha-dispensation as the child of an eminent brahmin at Sāvatthī, and named Muttā. And in her twentieth year, her destiny being fully ripe, she renounced the world under the Great Pajāpatī the Gotamid, and studied the exercises for ecstatic insight. Returning one day from her round for alms, she discharged her duties toward her seniors, and then going apart to rest, and seated out of sight, she began to concentrate herself. Then the Master, sitting in the 'Fragrant Chamber'[82] of the Vihāra, sent forth glory, and revealing himself as if seated before her, uttered the verse above. And she, steadfast in that exhortation, not long after attained Arahantship, and so attaining, exulted in the words of that verse. Completing her studies and promoted to full rank, she yet again uttered it, when about to pass away.

III
Puṇṇā.

The following verse is that of a student named Puṇṇā.[83] She, heaping up good of age-enduring efficacy under former Buddhas in this and that state of becoming, was born–when the world was empty of a Saviour Buddha–as a fairy, by the River Candabhāgā.[84] One day she worshipped a certain Silent [85] Buddha with a wreath of reeds. Thereby gaining heaven, she was, in this Buddha-dispensation, reborn as the child of a leading burgess of Sāvatthi and named Puṇṇā. When she had so dwelt for twenty years, her destiny then being fully ripe, she heard the Great Pajāpatī teach the doctrine, and renounced the world. Becoming a student, she began to practise insight. And the Master from the 'Fragrant Chamber' shed a glory, and spake this verse:

> Fill up, Puṇṇā,[86] the orb of holy life,
> E'en as on fifteenth day the full-orb'd moon.
> Fill full the perfect knowledge of the Path,
> And scatter all the gloom of ignorance.[87] (3)

Hearing this, her insight grew, and she attained Arahantship. This verse is the expression of her exultation and the affirmation of her AÑÑĀ.[88]

IV
Tissā.

The following verse is that of Tissā, a student. Heaping up merit under former Buddhas, Tissā was, in this Buddha-dispensation, reborn at Kapilavatthu in the noble clan of the Sākiyas. Made a lady of the Bodhisat's court, she renounced the world with Great Pajāpatī the Gotamid, and practised herself in insight. To her the Master appeared as to the foregoing Sisters, and said:

O Tissā! train thyself in the trainings three.
See that the great conjuncture [89] now at hand
Pass thee not by! Unloose all other yokes,
And fare thou forth purged of the deadly Drugs. [90](4)

And she, when she heard the verse, increased in insight, and attained Arahantship. Thereafter she was wont to repeat the lines.

V-X
Another Sister Tissā.

Tissā! lay well upon thy heart the yoke
Of noblest culture. See the moment come!
Let it not pass thee by! for many they
Who mourn in misery that moment past. (5)

Dhīrā.

Come, O Dhīrā, reach up and touch the goal
Where all distractions cease, where sense is stilled,
Where dwelleth bliss; win thou Nibbana, win
That sure Salvation [91] which hath no beyond. (6)

Another Sister Dhīrā.

Dhīrā, brave [92] Sister! who hath valiantly
Thy faculties in noblest culture trained,
Bear to this end thy last incarnate frame,
For thou hast conquered Māra and his host. (7)

Mittā.

Mittā, thou Sister friend! [93]who camest forth
Convinced in heart, love thou in thought and deed
Friends worthy of thy love. [94]So train thyself
In ways of good to win the safe, sure Peace. (8)

Bhadrā.

Bhadrā, who camest forth convinced in heart,
To sure felicity, O fortunate![95]
That heart devote. Develop [96] all that's good,
Faring to uttermost Security. (9)

Upasamā.

Upasamā! cross thou serene and calm [97]
The raging difficult Flood where death doth reign.
Bear to this end thy last incarnate frame,
For thou hast vanquished Māra and his host. (10)

Of all these six Sisters the story is similar to that of Tissā (IV.), with this exception: Dhīrā, called 'another Sister Dhīrā,' had no glory-verse pronounced to her, but was troubled in heart at the Master's teaching. Leaning on his words, she strove for insight, and when she had reached Arahantship, she declaimed her verse in exultation. All the others did the same.

THRESHING RICE IN 'MORTAR,' BANDIPUR, KASHMIR.

XI
Muttā[98]

Muttā, heaping up good under former Buddhas, was, in this Buddha-dispensation, born in the land of Kosala as the daughter of a poor brahmin named Oghāṭaka. Come to proper age, she was given to a hunchbacked brahmin; but she told him she could not continue in the life of the house, and induced him to consent to her leaving the world. Exercising herself in insight, her thoughts still ran on external objects of interest. So she practised self-control, and, repeating her verse, strove after insight till she won Arahantship; then exulting, she repeated:

> O free, indeed! O gloriously free
> Am I in freedom from three crooked things:–
> From quern, from mortar, from my crookback'd lord! [99]
> Ay, but I'm free from rebirth and from death,
> And all that dragged me back is hurled away. (11)

XII
Dhammadinnā.

Now, she, in the time when Padumuttara was Buddha, lived at Haŋsavatī in a state of servitude; and because she ministered and did honour to one of the chief apostles when he rose from his cataleptic trance, she was reborn in heaven and so on, among gods and men, till Phussa was Buddha. Then she worked merit by doubling the gift prescribed by her husband to the Master's half-brothers while they were staying in a servant's house. And when Kassapa was Buddha, she came to birth in the house of Kiki, King of Kāsī, as one of the Seven Sisters, his daughters,[100] and for 20,000 years lived a holy life. . . . Finally, in this Buddha-dispensation, she was reborn of a clansman's family at Rājagaha, and became the wife of Visākha, a leading citizen. Now one day her husband went to hear the Master teaching, and became One-who-returns-no-more. When he came home, Dhammadinnā met him as he went up the stairs; but he leant not on her outstretched hand, nor spoke to her at supper. And she asked: 'Dear sir, why did you not take my hand? Why do you not talk to me? Have I done anything amiss?' ''Tis for no fault in you, Dhammadinnā; but from henceforth I am not fit to touch a woman or take pleasure in food, for of such is the doctrine now borne in upon me. Do you according as you wish, either continuing to dwell here, or taking as much wealth as you need and going back to your family.' 'Nay, dear sir, I will make no such goings back. Suffer me to leave the world.' 'It is well, Dhammadinnā,' replied Visākha, and sent her to the Bhikkhunīs in a golden palanquin. Admitted to the Order, she shortly after asked permission of her teachers to go into retreat, saying: 'Mothers, my heart hath no delight in a place of crowds; I would go into a village abode.' The Bhikkhunīs brought her thither, and while there, because in her past lives she had subjugated the complexities of thought, word, and deed, she soon attained Arahantship, together with thorough mastery of the form and meaning of the Dhamma.[101] Thereupon she thought: 'Now have I reached the summit. What shall I do here any longer? I will even go to Rājagaha and worship the Master, and many of my kinsfolk will, through me, acquire merit.' So she returned with her Bhikkhunīs. Then Visākha, hearing of her return, curious to know why she came, interviewed her with questions on the Khandhas and the like. And Dhammadinnā answered every question as one might cut a lotus-stalk with a knife, and finally referred him to the Master. The Master praised her great wisdom, as it is told in the Lesser Vedalla (Miscellany) Sutta,[102] and ranked her foremost among the Sisters who could preach.

But it was while she was dwelling in the country, and, while yet in the lowest path, was acquiring insight to reach the highest, that she uttered her verse:

> In whom desire to reach the final rest
> Is born suffusing all the mind of her,
> Whose heart by lure of sense-desire no more
> Is held–BOUND UPSTREAM:–so shall she be called.[103]
> (12)

XIII
Visākhā.

Her story is similar to that of the Sister Dhīrā.[104] After winning Arahantship she pondered on the bliss of emancipation, and thus announced AÑÑĀ:

> The Buddha's will be done! See that ye do
> His will. An ye have done it, never more
> Need ye repent the deed. Wash, then, in haste
> Your feet and sit ye down aloof; alone.[105] (13)

Thus she admonished others to follow her example.

XIV
Sumanā.

Her story is similar to that of Sister Tissā.[106] Sending forth glory, the Master revealed himself as if seated in front of her, and spake:

Hast thou not seen sorrow and ill in all
The springs of life? Come thou not back to birth!
Cast out the passionate desire again to Be.
So shalt thou go thy ways calm and serene. (14)

XV
Uttarā.

Her story is also similar to that of Sister Tissā.[107] And it was the 'Glory-verse' through which she won Arahantship that she declaimed in exultation:

Well have I [108] disciplined myself in act,
In speech and eke in thought, rapt and intent.
Craving with root of craving [109] is o'ercome;
Cool am I now; I know Nibbana's peace. [110](15)

XVI
Sumanā

(Who left the world when old).

She too, having made her resolve under former Buddhas, and heaping up good in this life and in that, was, in this Buddha-dispensation, born at Sāvatthī as the sister of the King of Kosala.

Hearing the Master preach the doctrine to the King Pasenadi in the discourse beginning, 'There are four young creatures, sire, who may not be disregarded,' [111] she believed, and was established in the Refuges and the Precepts. Fain to leave the world, she put off doing so that she might take care of her grandmother as long as she lived. After the grandmother's death, Sumanā went, accompanied by the King, to the Vihāra, taking much treasure in carpets and shawls, and presenting them to the Order. And hearing the Master teach, she attained the fruit of the Path of No-return, and asked for ordination. And the Master, discerning the maturity of her knowledge, spake thus:

> Happily rest, thou venerable dame!
> Rest thee, wrapt in the robe thyself hast made.
> Stilled are the passions that have raged within.
> Cool art thou now, knowing Nibbana's peace. (16)

And when he had finished, she won Arahantship, together with thorough knowledge of the Norm in form and in meaning. [112]In her exultation she uttered that same verse, so that it became the announcement of her AÑÑĀ. Straightway she left the world for the Order.

XVII
Dhammā.

She, too, having made her resolve under former Buddhas, and heaping up merit in this and that state of becoming, was, in this Buddha-dispensation, born in a respectable family at Sāvatthī. Given in marriage to a suitable husband, she became converted, and desired to leave the world, but her husband would not consent. So she waited till after his death, and then entered the Order. One day, returning to the Vihāra from seeking alms, she lost her balance and fell. Making just that her base of insight, she won Arahantship with thorough knowledge of the Norm in form and in meaning. [113]And, triumphing, she uttered this verse:

Far had I wandered for my daily food;
Weary with shaking limbs I reached my rest,
Leaning upon my staff, when even there
I fell to earth.–Lo! all the misery
Besetting this poor mortal frame lay bare
To inward vision. [114]Prone the body lay;
The heart of me rose up in liberty. (17)

XVIII
Sanghā.

Her story is like that of Sister Dhīrā, [115]but her verse is as follows:

Home have I left, for I have left my world!
Child have I left, and all my cherish'd herds!
Lust have I left, and Ill-will, too, is gone,
And Ignorance have I put far from me;
Craving and root of Craving overpowered,
Cool am I now, knowing Nibbana's peace. (18)

PSALMS OF TWO VERSES

XIX
Abhirūpa-Nandā.

BORN in the time of the Buddha Vipassi, in his native town of Bandhumatī, as the daughter of a wealthy burgess, she became a pious lay-adherent, and at the Master's death she made an offering to the shrine of his ashes of a golden umbrella [116] surrounded with jewels. Reborn for this in various heavens, she was, in this Buddha-dispensation, reborn at Kapilavatthu as the daughter of the chief wife of Khemaka, the Sākiyan, and named Nandā. But because of her excessive beauty, charm, and loveliness, she was known as Nandā the Fair.

Now, on the day when she was to choose among her suitors,[117] Carabhūta, her young Sākiyan kinsman, died. Then her parents made her leave the world against her will. But she, even after she had entered the Order, was infatuated with her own beauty, and, fearing the Master's rebuke, avoided his presence. Now the Exalted One knew that she was ripe for knowledge, and directed the Great Pajājatī to let all the Bhikkhunīs come to him for instruction. Nandā sent another in her place. And the Exalted One said, 'Let no one come by proxy.' So she was compelled to come. And the Exalted One, by his mystic power, conjured up a beautiful woman, and showed her becoming aged and fading, causing anguish to arise in Nandā. And he addressed her in these words:

Behold, Nandā, the foul compound, diseased,

Impure! Compel thy heart to contemplate
What is not fair to view. So steel thyself
And concentrate the well-composèd mind. (19)
That ponder where no Threefold Sign [118] is seen.
Cast out the baneful bias of conceit.
Hath the mind mastered vain imaginings, [119]
Then mayst thou go thy ways, calm and serene. (20)

And when he had finished speaking, she attained Arahantship. Repeating to herself the verses, she made them the announcement of her AÑÑĀ.

XX
Jentī (or Jentā).

The story of her past and present is like that of Nandā the Fair; but it was at Vesālī, in the princely family of the Licchavis, that she was reborn. [120]There is this further difference: she attained Arahantship after hearing the Master preach the Dhamma, and it was when reflecting on the change that had come over her that she, in joy, uttered these verses:

The Seven Factors of the awakened mind[121]–
Seven ways whereby we may Nibbana win–
All, all have I developed and made ripe,
Even according to the Buddha's word. (21)
For I therein have seen as with mine eyes
The Bless'd, the Exalted One.[122] Last of all lives
Is this that makes up Me. The round of births
Is vanquishèd–Ne'er shall I be again! (22)

XXI
Sumangala's Mother.

She, too, having made her resolve under former Buddhas, and heaping up good in this rebirth and that, was born under this Buddha-dispensation in a poor family at Sāvatthī, and was married to a rush-plaiter. Her firstborn was a son, come for the last time to birth, who grew up to become the Elder Sumangala and an Arahant.[123] And her name not becoming known, she was called in the Pali text a certain unknown Therī, and is known as Sumangala's mother. She became a Bhikkhunī, and one day, while reflecting on all she had suffered as a laywoman, she was much affected, and, her insight quickening, she attained Arahantship, with thorough knowledge of the form and meaning of the Dhamma. Thereupon she exclaimed:

> O woman well set free! how free am I, [124]
> How throughly free from kitchen drudgery!
> Me stained and squalid 'mong my cooking-pots
> My brutal husband ranked as even less
> Than the sunshades he sits and weaves alway.[125] (23)
>
> Purged now of all my former lust and hate,
> I dwell, musing at ease beneath the shade
> Of spreading boughs–O, but 'tis well with me! (24)

XXII
Aḍḍhakāsī.

Born of a respectable family, in the time of Kassapa Buddha, she won understanding, and became a Bhikkhunī, established in the precepts. But she reviled an Arahant Elder Sister by calling her a prostitute,[126] and for this she went to purgatory. In this Buddha-dispensation she was reborn in the kingdom of Kāsī as the child of a distinguished and prosperous citizen. But because of the persistent effect of her former evil speech, she became herself a prostitute. How she left the world and was ordained by special messenger is related in the Culla Vagga. [127]For she wished to go to Sāvatthī to be ordained by the Exalted One. But the libertines of Benares barred the ways, so she sent and asked the Exalted One's advice, and he permitted her to be ordained by a messenger. Then she, working at insight, not long after obtained Arahantship, with thorough knowledge of the Dhamma in form and meaning. Thereupon she exclaimed:

No less my fee was than the Kāsī realm
Paid in revènue–this was based on that,
Value for value,–so the sheriff fixed. (25)

But irksome now is all my loveliness;
I weary of it, disillusionized.
Ne'er would I more, again and yet again,
Run on the round of rebirth and of death!
Now real and true for me the Triple Lore.[128]
Accomplished is the bidding of the Lord. (26)

XXIII
Cittā.

She, too, having made her resolve under former Buddhas, and heaping up good of age-enduring efficacy in this rebirth and that, was born in the 94th æon [129] as a fairy. She worshipped with offering of flowers a Silent (Pacceka) Buddha. [130]And after many other births among men and gods, she was, in this Buddha-dispensation, born at Rājagaha in the family of a leading burgess. When she had come to years of discretion she heard the Master teaching at the gate of Rājagaha, and, becoming a believer, she was ordained by the Great Pajāpatī the Gotamid. And at length, in her old age, when she had climbed the Vulture's Peak, and had done the exercises of a recluse, her insight expanded, and she won to Arahantship. Reflecting thereon, she gave utterance as follows:

Though I be suffering and weak, and all
My youthful spring be gone, yet have I climbed,
Leaning upon my staff, the mountain crest. (27)
Thrown from my shoulder hangs my cloak, o'erturned
My little bowl. So 'gainst the rock I lean
And prop this self of me, and break away
The wildering gloom that long had closed me in. (28)

XXIV
Mettikā.

Heaping up merit under former Buddhas, she was born during the time of Siddhattha, [131]the Exalted One, in a burgess's family, and worshipped at his shrine by offering there a jewelled girdle. After many births in heaven and on earth, through the merit thereof, she became, in this Buddha-dispensation, the child of an eminent brahmin at Rājagaha. In other respects her case is like the preceding one, save that it was another hill corresponding to Vulture's Peak up which she climbed. [132]

She, too, reflecting on what she had won, said in exultation:

Though I be suffering and weak, and all
My youthful spring be gone, yet have I come,
Leaning upon my staff, and clomb aloft
The mountain peak. (29)
            My cloak thrown off,
My little bowl o'erturned: so sit I here
Upon the rock. And o'er my spirit sweeps
The breath [133] of Liberty! I win, I win
The Triple Lore! The Buddha's will is done!(30)

THE GIJJHAKŪṬI (VULTURE PEAK) RANGE ABOVE OLD RĀJAGAHA.

XXV
Mittā.[134]

Born in the time of Vipassi Buddha of a noble family, and become a lady of his father's court, she won meritorious karma by bestowing food and precious raiment on an Arahant Elder Sister. [135]Born finally, in this Buddha-dispensation, in the princely family of the Sākiyas, at Kapilavatthu, she left the world together with Great Pajāpatī the Gotamid, and, going through the requisite training for insight, not long after won Arahantship.

Reflecting thereon, joy and gladness stirred her to say:

On full-moon day and on the fifteenth day,
And eke the eighth of either half the month,
I kept the feast; I kept the precepts eight,
The extra fasts, [136]enamoured of the gods,
And fain to dwell in homes celestial. (31)

To-day one meal, head shaved, a yellow robe–
Enough for me. I want no heaven of gods.
Heart's pain, heart's pining, have I trained away. (32)

XXVI
Abhayā's Mother.

Heaping up merit under former Buddhas, she, in the time of Tissa Buddha,[137] saw him going round for alms, and with glad heart took his bowl and placed in it a spoonful of food. Reborn for that among gods and among men, she was born also for that, in this Buddha-dispensation, and became the town belle of Ujjenī, by name Padumavatī.[138] And King Bimbisāra (of Magadha) heard of her, and expressed to his chaplain the wish to see her. By the power of his spells, the chaplain summoned a Yakkha who, by his might, brought the King to Ujjenī. And when she afterwards sent word to the King that she was with child by him, he sent back word, saying: 'If it be a son, let me see him when he is grown.' And she bore a son and called him Abhaya. When he was seven years old she told him who was his father, and sent him to Bimbisāra. The King loved the boy, and let him grow up with the boys of his court. His conversion and ordination is told in the Psalms of the Elders.[139] And, later on, his mother heard her son preach the Dhamma, and she, too, left the world and afterwards attained Arahantship, with thorough grasp of the Dhamma in form and meaning. She thereupon recalled and repeated the verse wherewith her son had admonished her, and added her own thereto:

'Upward from sole of foot, O mother dear,
Downward from crown of hair this body see.
Is't not impure, the evil-smelling thing?' (33)
This have I pondered. meditating still,
Till every throb of lust is rooted out.
Expunged is all the fever of desire.

Cool am I now and calm–Nibbana's peace. (34)

XXVII
Abhayā.[140]

She, too, having made her resolve under former Buddhas, and heaping up merit of age-enduring efficacy in this and that state of becoming, was, in the time of Sikhi Buddha,[141] reborn in a great noble's family, and became the chief queen of his father Aruṇa. And one day she worshipped the Exalted One with offering of red lotuses given her by the King, when Sikhi Buddha, at alms-time, entered the palace. Reborn for this among gods and men, she was, in this Buddha-dispensation, born once more at Ujjenī in a respectable family, and became the playmate of Abhaya's mother. And when the latter had left the world, Abhayā, for love of her, also took orders. Dwelling with her at Rājagaha, she went one day to Cool-Grove to contemplate on a basis of some foul thing.[142] The Master, seated in his Fragrant Chamber, caused her to see before her the kind of object she had been directed to choose. Seeing the vision, dread seized her. Then the Master, sending forth glory, appeared as if seated before her, and said:

Brittle, O Abhayā, the body is,
Whereto the worldling's happiness is bound.
For me I shall lay down this mortal frame,
Mindful and self-possessed in all I do. (35)
For all my heart was in the work whereby
I struggled free from all that breedeth Ill.
Craving have I destroyed, and brought to pass
That which the Buddhas have revealed to men.[143] (36)

And when he had finished speaking she attained Arahantship. Exulting herein, she turned the verses round into an address to herself.

XXVIII
Sāmā.

She, too, having made her resolve under former Buddhas, and heaping up good of age-enduring efficacy in this and that state of becoming, being reborn in fortunate conditions, took birth, in this Buddha-dispensation, at Kosambī, in the family of an eminent burgess. When her dear friend, the lay-disciple Sāmāvatī, died, she, in her distress, left the world. But being unable to subdue her grief for her friend, she was unable to grasp the Ariyan Way. Now, while she was seated in the sitting-room, listening to Elder Ānanda preaching, she was established in insight, and, on the seventh day after, attained Arahantship, with thorough grasp of the Dhamma in form and meaning.

And reflecting on what she had won, she expressed it in this psalm:

> Four times, nay, five, I sallied from my cell,
> And roamed afield to find the peace of mind
> I sought in vain, and governance of thoughts
> I could not bring into captivity. [144](37)
> To me, even to me, on that eighth day
> It came: all craving ousted from my heart.
> 'Mid many sore afflictions, I had wrought
> With passionate endeavour, and had won!
> Craving was dead, and the Lord's will was done. (38)

PSALMS OF THREE VERSES

XXIX
Another Sāmā.

SHE also, heaping up good like the foregoing, was born, in the time of Vipassi Buddha, as a fairy on the banks of the River Candabhāgā.[145] Devoted to fairy pastimes, she saw one day the Master walking on the bank, that he might sow the good seed among creatures. And with great glee she wor-shipped, offering flowers.[146] For this she gained rebirth among gods and men, till, in this Buddha-dispensation, she took birth in a clansman's family at Kosambī. She too became the friend of Sāmāvatī, and she too, out of grief at the death of the latter, entered the Order. She too could not gain self-mastery for twenty-five years, till in her old age she heard a timely sermon, through which her insight expanded and she won Arahantship, with thorough grasp of the Dhamma in form and meaning. Thereon reflecting, she broke forth:

Full five-and-twenty years since I came forth!
But in my troubled heart in no way yet
Could I discern the calm of victory. (39)
The peace of mind, the governance of thoughts
Long sought, I found not; and with anguish thrilled
I dwelt in memory on the Conqueror's word.[147] (40)
To free my path from all that breedeth Ill
I strove with passionate ardour, and I won!
Craving is dead, and the Lord's will is done.
To-day is now the seventh day since first
Was withered up within that ancient Thirst. (41)

XXX
Uttamā.

She, too, heaping up good under former Buddhas, was in the time of Vipassi Buddha, born at Bandhumatī, in the house of a certain wealthy landowner, and became a domestic servant. Grown up, she tended her master's household. Now, at that time, King Bandhumā (Vipassi's father), having restored Sabbath-keeping, gave gifts before dining and, after dining, attended a sermon; and the people, following his pious example, and keeping Sabbath, the slave thought: 'Why should not I, too, do as they all are doing?' And for the thoroughness of her observance of the feasts she was reborn among the Three-and-Thirty gods, and in other happy realms, and finally, in this Buddha-era, in the house of the Treasurer of Sāvatthī. Come to years of discretion, she heard Paṭācārā preach, and entered the Order; but she was unable to attain the climax of insight till Paṭācārā,[148] seeing the state of her mind, gave her admonition. Thereby established, she won Arahantship, with thorough grasp of the Norm in form and in meaning. And reflecting thereon, she exulted thus:

Four times, nay, five, I sallied from my cell,
And roamed afield to find the peace of mind
Long vainly sought, and governance of thoughts
I could not bring into captivity. (42)
To me she came, that noble Bhikkhunī,
Who was my foster-mother in the faith–
She taught to me the Norm, wherein I learnt
The nature of this transitory self.[149] (43)
And well I minded all, e'en as she taught.
For seven days I sat in Jhāna-joy
And ease, cross-legged; on the eighth day at last
I stretched my limbs, and went my way serene,

For I had burst asunder the surrounding gloom. (44)

Now, this was the affirmation of her AÑÑĀ.

XXXI
Another Uttamā.

She, too, having made her resolve under former Buddhas, and heaping up good of age-enduring efficacy in this and that rebirth, was born, in the time of Vipassi Buddha, as a domestic servant, at Bandhumatī. One day, seeing an Arahant of the Master's Order seeking alms, she gladly offered him three sweet cakes. Through this reborn to happiness, she finally came to birth, in this Buddha-era, in the family of an eminent brahmin in the country of Kosala. Come to years of discretion, she heard the Master preach while touring in the country, and leaving the world, she soon won Arahantship, together with thorough grasp of the Norm in form and in meaning. And reflecting thereon, she exulted thus:

The Seven Factors of the Awakened mind–[150]
Seven Ways whereby we may Nibbana win–
All, all have I developed and made ripe,
Even according to the Buddha's word. (45)
Fulfilled is heart's desire: I win the Void,
I win the Signless![151] Buddha's daughter I,
Born of his mouth, his blessed word, I stand,
Transported with Nibbana's bliss alway. (46)
And all the sense-desires that fetter gods,
That hinder men, are wholly riven off.
Abolished is the infinite round of births.
Becoming cometh ne'er again for me. (47)

XXXII
Dantikā.

She, too, having made her resolve under former Buddhas, and in this and that rebirth heaping up good of age-enduring efficacy, was born, when the world was empty of a Buddha, as a fairy by the River Candabhāgā.[152] Sporting one day with the fairies, and straying awhile, she saw a silent Buddha seated at the foot of a tree, and adored him in faith with flower-offerings. For this she was reborn among gods and men, and, finally, in this Buddha-era, at Sāvatthī, in the house of the King's chaplain-brahmin. Come to years of discretion, she became a lay-believer in the Jeta Grove [College], and, later, entered the Order under Great Pajāpatī the Gotamid. And one day, while staying at Rājagaha, she ascended the Vulture's Peak, after her meal, and while resting, she saw that which she tells of in her verse, whereby she won Arahantship, with thorough grasp of the Norm in form and in meaning. And afterwards, thrilled with happiness at the thought of her attainment, she exulted thus:

Coming from noonday-rest on Vulture's Peak,
I saw an elephant, his bathe performed,
Forth from the river issue. And a man, (48)
Taking his goad, bade the great creature [153] stretch
His foot: 'Give me thy foot!' The elephant
Obeyed, and to his neck the driver sprang. (49)
I saw the untamed tamed, [154]I saw him bent
To master's will; and marking inwardly,
I passed into the forest depths and there
I' faith I trained and ordered all my heart. (50)

XXXIII
Ubbirī.

She too, having made her resolve in the time of former Buddhas, and heaping up, in this and that rebirth, Good valid for an æon of evolution, was born, in the time of Padumuttara

Buddha, at the town of Haŋsavatī in a clansman's house. Come to years of discretion, she was left alone one day, her parents being engaged with a party in the inner court of the house. And seeing an Arahant approaching the house-door, she bade him 'Come in hither, lord,' and did him homage, showing him to a seat; she then took his bowl and filled it with food. The Elder thanked her, and departed. But she, reborn therefore in the heaven of the Three-and-Thirty gods, enjoying there a heavenly time and many a happy life thereafter, was, in this Buddha-era, reborn at Sāvatthī in the family of a very eminent burgess. And she was beautiful to see, and was brought into the house of the King of Kosala himself.[155] After a few years a daughter was born to her, whom she named Jīvā.[156] The King saw the child, and was so pleased that he had Ubbirī anointed as Queen. But anon the little girl died, and the mother went daily mourning to the charnel-field. And one day she went and worshipped the Master, and sat down; but soon she left, and stood lamenting by the River Achiravatī. Then the Master, seeing her from afar, revealed himself, and asked her: 'Why dost thou weep?' 'I weep because of my daughter, Exalted One.' 'Burnt in this cemetery are some 84,000 [157] of thy daughters. For which of them dost thou weep?' And pointing out the place where this one and that one had been laid, he said half the psalm:

O Ubbirī, who wailest in the wood,
Crying 'O Jīvā! O my daughter dear!'
Come to thyself! Lo, in this burying-ground
Are burnt full many a thousand daughters dear,
And all of them were named like unto her.
Now which of all those Jīvās dost thou mourn? (51)

And she pondered with intelligence on the Norm thus taught by the Master, and so stirred up insight that, by the charm of his teaching and her own attainment of the requisite conditions, she reached the topmost fruit, even Arahantship.[158] And showing forth the high distinction she had won, she spoke the second half of the psalm:

Lo! from my heart the hidden shaft is gone!
The shaft that nestled there hath he removed.
And that consuming grief for my dead child
Which poisoned all the life of me is dead. (52)
To-day my heart is healed, my yearning stayed,
And all within is purity and peace. [159]
Lo! I for refuge to the Buddha go–
The only wise–the Order and the Norm. [160](53)

XXXIV
Sukkā.

She, too, having fared in the past as the foregoing Sisters, was born in a clansman's house. [161]Come to years of discretion, she went with lay-women disciples to the Vihāra, [162]and heard the Master preach. Becoming a believer, she left the world and became learned, proficient in the doctrine, and a ready speaker. Leading for centuries a religious life, [163]she yet died a worldling at heart, and was reborn in the heaven of bliss.[164] Again, when Vipassi was Buddha, and again when Vessabhu was Buddha, she kept the precepts, and was learned and proficient in doctrine. Again, when Kakusandha was Buddha, and yet again when Konāgamana was Buddha, she took Orders, and was pure in conduct, learnèd, and a preacher. At length, she was, in this Buddha-era, reborn at Rājagaha, in the family of an eminent burgess, and called Sukkā (bright, lustrous, 'Lucy'). Come to years of discretion, she found faith in the Master at her own home, and became a lay-disciple. But later, when she heard Dhammadinnā preach,[165] she was thrilled with emotion, and renounced the world under her. And performing the exercises for insight, she not long after attained Arahantship, together with thorough grasp of the Norm in form and in meaning.

Thereupon, attended by 500 Bhikkhunīs, she became a great preacher. And one day, when they had been into Rājagaha for alms, and had returned and dined, they entered the Bhikkhunīs' settlement, and Sukkā, with a great company seated around her, taught the doctrine in such wise that she seemed to be giving them sweet mead to drink and sprinkling them with ambrosia. And they all listened to her rapt, motionless, intent. Thereupon the spirit[166] of the tree that stood at the end of the Sisters' terrace was inspired by her teaching, and went out to Rājagaha, walking about the ways and the squares proclaiming her excellence, and saying:

What would ye men of Rājagaha have?
What have ye done? that mute and idle here
Ye lie about, as if bemused with wine,
Nor wait upon Sukkā, while she reveals
The precious gospel by the Buddha taught. (54)
The wise in heart, methinks, were fain to quaff
That life's elixir, once won never lost,
That welleth ever up in her sweet words,
E'en as the wayfarer welcomes the rain. (55)

And hearing what the tree-spirit said, the people were excited, and came to the Sister and listened attentively.

At a later period, when the Sister, at the end of her life, was completing her Nibbana, and wished to show how the system she had taught led to salvation, she declared her AÑÑĀ thus:

O Child of light![167] by light of truth set free
From cravings dire, firm, self-possessed, serene,

Bear to this end thy last incarnate frame,
For thou hast conquered Mara and his host. (56)

THE SITE OF 'NEW' RĀJAGAHA, BUILT BY BIMBISĀRA.

XXXV
Selā.

She, too, having fared in the past as the foregoing Sisters, was born in a clansman's house at Haŋsavatī, [168]and was given in marriage by her parents to a clansman's son of equal birth. With him she lived happily till his death. Then, being herself advanced in years, and growing anxious as she sought to find Good, [169]she went about from park to park, [170]from vihāra to vihāra, with the intention of teaching religion (dhamma) to votaries of religion. Then one day she came up to the Bo-tree of the Master [171] and sat down, thinking: 'If a Buddha, an Exalted One, be unequalled and peerless among men, may this one show me the miracle of Buddhahood.' Scarce had the thought arisen when the Tree blazed forth, the branches appeared as if made of gold, the horizon shone all around. And she, inspired at that sight, fell down and worshipped, and for seven days sat there. On the seventh day she performed a grand feast of offering and worship to the Buddha.[172] By this meritorious karma she was reborn in this Buddha-era, in the kingdom of Āḷavī, as the King's daughter, and named Selā. [173]But she was also known as 'The Āḷavikan.' [174] Come to years of discretion, the Master converted her father, ordained him, and went with him to the city of Āḷavī. Selā, being yet unmarried, went with the King and heard the Master preach. She became a believer and a lay-disciple. Afterwards, growing anxious, she took Orders, worked her way to insight, and because of the promise in her and the maturity of her knowledge, she, crushing the formations of thought, word and deed,[175] soon won Arahantship.

Thereafter, as an Elder, she lived at Sāvatthī. And one day she went forth from Sāvatthī to take siesta in the Dark Grove, and sat down beneath a tree. Then Māra, alone and wishing to interrupt her privacy, approached in the guise of a stranger, saying:

> Ne'er shalt thou find escape while in the world!
> What profiteth thee then thy loneliness?
> Take the good things of life while yet thou mayst.
> Repentance else too late awaiteth thee. (57)

Then the Sister–thinking: 'Verily, 'tis that foolish Māra who would deny me the Nibbana that is revealed to me, and bids me choose the sensuous life. He knows not that I am an Arahant. Now will I tell him and confound him'– recited the following: [176]

> Like spears and javelins are the joys of sense
> That pierce and rend the mortal frames of us.
> These that thou callest 'the good things of life'–
> Good of that ilk to me is nothing worth. (58)

> On every hand the love of pleasure yields,
> And the thick gloom of ignorance is rent
> In twain. Know this, O Evil One, avaunt!

Here, O Destroyer, shalt thou not prevail. (59)

XXXVI
Somā. [177]

She, too, having fared in the past as the foregoing Sisters, was, in the time of Sikhi Buddha, [178]reborn in the family of an eminent noble, and, when grown up, was made the chief consort of the King Aruṇavā. The story of her past is similar to that of Sister Abhayā. [179]The story of her present is that, in this Buddha-era, she was reborn as the daughter of the chaplain of King Bimbisāra [180]at Rājagaha, and named Somā. Come to years of discretion, she came to believe in the Master in her own home, and became a lay-disciple. And later on, growing anxious, she entered the Order of Bhikkhunīs, and, working her way to insight, she not long after won Arahantship, with thorough grasp of the Norm in letter and in spirit.

Then, dwelling at Sāvatthī in the bliss of emancipation, she went forth one day to take siesta in the Dark Grove, and sat down beneath a tree. And Māra, alone, and wishing to interrupt her privacy, approached her, invisible and in the air, saying:

That vantage-ground the sages may attain is hard
To reach. With her two-finger consciousness
That is no woman competent to gain! (60)

For women, from the age of seven or eight, boiling rice at all times, know not the moment when the rice is cooked, but must take some grains in a spoon and press it with two fingers; hence the expression 'two-finger' sense. [181]Then the Elder rebuked Māra:

How should the woman's nature hinder us?
Whose hearts are firmly set, who ever move

With growing knowledge onward in the Path?
What can that signify to one in whom
Insight doth truly comprehend the Norm? [182](61)
On every hand the love of pleasure yields,
And the thick gloom of ignorance is rent
In twain. Know this, O Evil One, avaunt!
Here, O Destroyer! shalt thou not prevail. (62)

PSALMS OF FOUR VERSES

XXXVII
Bhaddā of the Kapilas. [183]

NOW she was born in the time of Padumuttara Buddha, in a clansman's house at Haŋsavatī. Come to years of discretion, she heard the Master preach, and saw him assign a Bhikkhunī the first rank among those who could recall previous lives. Thereat she made her resolve, wishing that she, too, might acquire such a rank. Working merit all her life, she was reborn, when no Buddha had arisen, in a clansman's house at Benares, and in due course married.

Then one day a quarrel arose between her and her sister-in-law. And the latter having given food to a Silent Buddha, Bhaddā thought, 'She will win glory for this,' and taking the bowl from his hand, she filled it with mud instead of food. The people said, 'Foolish woman! what has the Silent Buddha done to offend you?' And she, ashamed of herself, took back the bowl, emptied and scrubbed it with scented powder, filled it with the four sweet foods, and sprinkled it on the top with ghee of the colour of a lotus-calyx. Handing it back, shining, to the Silent Buddha, she registered a prayer: 'May I have a shining body like this bowl!'

After many fortunate rebirths, she was reborn, in the time of Kassapa Buddha, at Benares, as the daughter of the wealthy treasurer. But by the fruition of her previous karma her body was of evil odour, and she was repulsive to others. Much troubled thereby, she had her ornaments made into an ingot of gold, and placed it in the Buddha's shrine, doing reverence with her hands full of lotuses. Thereby her body, even in that birth, became fragrant and sweet. As a beloved wife she did good all her life, was reborn in heaven to celestial joys, and at length took birth as the daughter of the King of Benares. There she lived gloriously, ministering to Silent Buddhas. When they passed away she was greatly troubled, and left the world for ascetic practices. Dwelling in groves, she practised Jhana, and was reborn in the Brahma heavens, and thence into the family of a brahmin of the Kosiya clan at Sāgala.[184] Reared in great state, she was wedded to the young noble Pippali at the village of Mahā-tittha. When he renounced the world she handed over her great wealth to her kinsfolk that she too might go forth; and she dwelt five years in the Sophists' Grove,[185] after which she was ordained by Great Pajāpatī the Gotamid. Establishing insight, she soon won Arahantship.

And she became an expert in knowledge of her past lives, through the surplus force of her resolve (made in past ages), and was herein ranked first by the Master when, seated in the Jeta Grove among the company of Ariyans,[186] he classified the Bhikkhunīs. One day she broke forth in a Psalm, recounting all that she had wrought, accompanied by a eulogy of the virtues of the great Elder Kassapa, [187]thus:

> Son of the Buddha and his heir is he,
> Great Kassapa, master of self, serene!
> The vision of far, bygone days is his,
> Ay, heaven and hell no secrets hold for him. (63)
> Death too of rebirth hath he won, and eke
> A seer is he of mystic lore profound.
> By these three arms[188] of learning doth he stand
> Thrice-wise, 'mong gods and men elect, sublime. (64)

She too, Bhaddā the Kapilan–thrice-wise
And victor over death and birth is she–
Bears to this end her last incarnate frame,
For she hath conquered Mara and his host. (65)

We both have seen, both he and I, the woe
And pity of the world, and have gone forth.
We both are Arahants with selves well tamed.
Cool are we both, ours is Nibbana now! (66)

PSALMS OF FIVE VERSES

XXXVIII
An Anonymous Sister.

SHE, too, having fared in the past as the foregoing Sisters, was, in this Buddha-era, reborn in the town of Devadaha, and became the nurse of Great Pajāpatī the Gotamid. Her name was Vaḍḍhesī, but the name of her family has not been handed down. When her mistress renounced the world she did the same. But for five-and-twenty years she was harassed by the lusts of the senses, winning no concentration of mind even for a moment, and bewailing her state with outstretched arms, till at length she heard Dhammadinnā preaching the Norm. Then, with her mind diverted from the senses, she fell to practising meditative exercises, and in no long time acquired the Six Powers of Intuition. [189]And, reflecting on her attainment, she exulted thus:

For five-and-twenty years since I came forth,
Not for one moment could my heart attain
The blessedness of calm serenity. (67)
No peace of mind I found. My every thought
Was soaked in the fell drug of sense-desire. [190]
With outstretched arms and shedding futile tears
I gat me, wretched woman, to my cell. (68)

Then She to this poor Bhikkhunī drew near,
Who was my foster-mother in the faith.
She taught to me the Norm, wherein I learnt
The factors, organs, bases of this self,

Impermanent compound. [191]Hearing her words, (69)
Beside her I sat down to meditate.

And now I know the days of the long past,
And clearly shines the Eye Celestial, (70)
I know the thoughts of other minds, and hear
With sublimated sense the sound of things
Ineffable. [192]The mystic potencies
I exercise; and all the deadly Drugs
That poisoned every thought are purged away.
A living truth for me this Sixfold Lore,
And the commandment of the Lord is done. (71)

XXXIX
Vimalā.
(Formerly a Courtesan.)

She too, having fared in the past as the foregoing Sisters, was born, in this Buddha-era, at Vesālī as the daughter of a certain woman who earned her living by her beauty. Her name was Vimalā. When she was grown up, and was imagining vicious things, she saw one day the venerable Mahā-Moggallāna [193] going about Vesālī for alms, and feeling enamoured of him, she went to his dwelling and sought to entice him. Some say she was instigated to do so by sectarians. The Elder rebuked her unseemly behaviour and admonished her, as may be read in the Psalms of the Brethren. [194]And she was filled with shame and self-reproach, and became a believer and lay-sister. Later she entered the Order, and wrestling and striving–for the root of attainment was in her–not long after won Arahantship. Thereafter, reflecting on her gain, she exulted thus:

How was I once puff'd up, incens'd with the bloom of
my beauty, [195]

Vain of my perfect form, my fame and success 'midst the people,
Fill'd with the pride of my youth, unknowing the Truth and unheeding! (72)
Lo! I made my body, bravely arrayed, deftly painted,
Speak for me to the lads, whilst I at the door of the harlot
Stood, like a crafty hunter, weaving his snares, ever watchful. (73)
Yea, I bared without shame my body and wealth of adorning;
Manifold wiles I wrought, devouring the virtue of many. (74)

To-day with shaven head, wrapt in my robe,
I go forth on my daily round for food;
And 'neath the spreading boughs of forest tree
I sit, and Second-Jhana's rapture win,
Where reas'nings cease, and joy and ease remain. [196](75)
Now all the evil bonds that fetter gods
And men are wholly rent and cut away.
Purg'd are the Āsavas that drugg'd my heart,
Calm and content I know Nibbana's Peace. (76)

XL
Sīhā.

She too, faring in the past as the foregoing Sisters, was in this Buddha-era born at Vesālī as the daughter of General Sīha's [197] sister. And, being named after her maternal uncle, she was called Sīhā. Come to years of discretion, she heard the Master one day teaching the Norm to the General, and, becoming a believer, gained her parents' consent to enter the Order. When she strove for insight, she was unable to prevent her mind from running on objects of external charm. Harassed thus for seven years, she concluded, 'How shall I extricate myself from this evil living? I will die.' And, taking a noose, she hung it round the bough of a tree, and, fastening it round her neck, with all the cumulative effect of former efforts, she impelled her mind to insight. Then to her, who was really come to her last birth, at that very moment, through her knowledge attaining maturity, insight grew within, and she won Arahantship, together with thorough grasp of the Norm in form and in meaning. So, loosening the rope from her neck, she turned back again. Established as an Arahant, she exulted thus:

Distracted, harassed by desires of sense,
Unmindful of the 'what' and 'why' of things, [198]
Stung and inflated by the memories
Of former days, o'er which I lacked control– (77)
Corrupting canker spreading o'er my heart–
I followed heedless dreams of happiness,
And got no even tenour to my mind,
All given o'er to dalliance with sense. (78)
So did I fare for seven weary years,
In lean and sallow mis'ry of unrest.
I, wretched, found no ease by day or night, (79)
So took a rope and plunged into the wood:
'Better for me a friendly gallows-tree!
I'll live again the low life of the world.'[199] (80)
Strong was the noose I made; and on a bough
I bound the rope and flung it round my neck,
When see! . . . my heart was set at liberty! (81)

XLI
Sundarī-Nandā.

She, verily, was born, in the time of Padumuttara Buddha, in the town of Haŋsavatī. And when she was come to years of discretion, she heard the Master preaching, and assigning a certain Bhikkhunī the foremost place in meditative power. Vowing that she would gain that rank, she went on doing good. After æons upon æons of rebirth among gods and men, she took birth in this Buddha-epoch in the reigning family of the Sākiyas. Named Nandā, she became known as Beautiful Nandā, [200]the Belle of the country. And when our Exalted One had acquired all knowledge, had gone to Kapilavatthu, and caused the princes Nandā and Rāhula to join the Order; when too King Suddhodana died, and the Great Pajāpatī entered the Order, then Nandā thought: 'My elder brother [201] has renounced the heritage of empire, has left the world, and is become a Buddha, a Superman. [202]His son too, Rāhula, has left the world, so has my brother, King Nanda, my mother, Mahā-Pajāpatī, and my sister, Rāhula's mother. But I now, what shall I do at home? I will leave the world.' Thus she went forth, not from faith, but from love of her kin. And thus, even after her renunciation, she was intoxicated with her beauty, and would not go into the Master's presence, lest he should rebuke her. But it fared with her even as with Sister Abbirūpa-Nandā, [203]with this difference: When she saw the female shape conjured up by the Master growing gradually aged, her mind, intent on the impermanence and suffering of life, turned to meditative discipline. And the Master, seeing that, taught her suitable doctrine, thus:

> Behold, Nandā, the foul compound, diseased,
> Impure! Compel thy heart to contemplate
> What is not fair to view. So steel thyself
> And concentrate the well-composèd mind. [204](82)
> As with this body, so with thine; as with
> Thy beauty, so with this–thus shall it be
> With this malodorous, offensive shape,

Wherein the foolish only take delight. (83)
So look thou on it day and night with mind
Unfalteringly steadfast, till alone,
By thine own wit, delivered from the thrall
Of beauty, thou dost gain vision serene.[205] (84)

Then she, heeding the teaching, summoned up wisdom and stood firm in the fruition of the First Path. And, to give her an exercise for higher progress, he taught her, saying: 'Nandā, there is in this body not even the smallest essence. 'Tis but a heap of bones smeared with flesh and blood under the form of decay and death.' As it is said in the Dhammapada:[206]

'Have made a citadel of bones besmeared
With flesh and blood, where ever reign decay
And death, and where conceit and fraud is stored.

Then she, as he finished, attained Arahantship. And when she pondered on her victory, she exulted in the Master's words, and added:

I, even I, have seen, inside and out,
This body as in truth it really is,
Who sought to know the 'what' and 'why' of it,
With zeal unfaltering and ardour fired. (85)
Now for the body care I never more,
And all my consciousness is passion-free.
Keen with unfettered zeal, detached,
Calm and serene I taste Nibbana's peace. (86)

XLII
Nanduttarā.

She, too, faring in the past as the aforementioned Sisters, was, in this Buddha-age, born in the kingdom of the Kurus at the town of Kammāsadamma,[207] in a brahmin family. And when she had learnt from some of them their arts and sciences, she entered the Order of the Nigaṇṭhas,[208] and, as a renowned speaker, took her rose-apple bough, like Bhaddā Curlyhair, [209]and toured about the plain of India. Thus she met Mahā-Moggallāna the Elder, and in debate suffered defeat. She thereupon listened to his advice, entered the Order, and not long after attained Arahantship, together with thorough grasp of the letter and meaning of the Norm. And meditating on her victory, she exulted thus:

Fire and the moon, the sun and eke the gods
I once was wont to worship and adore,
Foregathering on the river-banks to go
Down in the waters for the bathing rites. (87)
Ay, manifold observances I laid
Upon me, for I shaved one-half my head,
Nor laid me down to rest save on the earth,
Nor ever broke my fast at close of day. (88)

I sought delight in decking out myself
With gems and ornaments and tricks of art.
By baths, unguents, massage, I ministered
Unto this body, spurred by lusts of sense. (89)

Then found I faith, and forth from home
I went into the homeless life, for I
Had seen the body as it really is,
And nevermore could lusts of sense return. (90)

All the long line of lives was snapt in twain,
Ay, every wish and yearning for it gone.
All that had tied me hand and foot was loosed,
Peace had I won, peace thronèd in my heart. (91)

XLIII
Mittakālī. [210]

She, too, faring in the past as the aforementioned Sisters, was, in this Buddha-era, born at the town of Kammāsadamma [211] in the kingdom of the Kurus, in a brahmin's family. Come to years of discretion, she gained faith by hearing the teaching of the great Discourse on the Applications of Mindfulness,[212] and entered the Order of Sisters. For seven years she was liable to a fondness for gifts and honours, and, while doing the duties of a recluse, she was quarrelsome now and again. Later on she was reborn intellectually, [213]and becoming anxious she established insight, and thereupon soon won Arahantship, together with thorough grasp of the Norm in form and in meaning. Reflecting on her victory, she exulted thus:

Leaving my home through call of faith, I sought
The homeless life, and dwelt with eye intent
On offerings from the faithful and the praise
Of this one and the gratitude of that. (92)
The path of insight [214] I neglected, turned
From highest good to follow baser ends.
I lay enthralled to worldly vice, and naught
To win the goal of my high calling wrought. (93)

But anguish crept upon me, even me,
Whenas I pondered in my little cell:
Ah me! how have I come into this evil road!
Into the power of Craving have I strayed! (94)
Brief is the span of life yet left to me;
Old age, disease, hang imminent to crush.
Now, ere this body perish and dissolve,
Swift let me be; no time have I for sloth. (95)
And contemplating, as they really are,

The Aggregates of life that come and go,
I rose and stood with mind emancipate!
For me the Buddha's word had come to pass. (96)

XLIV
Sakulā. [215]

Now she, at the time when Padumuttara was Buddha, came to birth at Haŋsavatī as the daughter of King Ānanda and half-sister of the Master, and was named Nandā. One day she sat listening to the Master, and hearing him place a Bhikkhunī at the top of those who had the faculty of the 'Heavenly Eye,' she vowed that this rank should one day be hers. And after many good works and subsequent happy rebirths, she came to being on earth when Kassapa was Buddha, as a brahminee, and renounced the world as a Wanderer, [216]vowed to a solitary life. One day she offered her alms at the Master's shrine, making a lamp-offering all night long. Reborn in the heaven of the Three-and-Thirty Gods, she became possessed of the Heavenly Eye; and, when this Buddha was living, she was born a brahminee at Sāvatthī, and called Pakulā. Assisting at the Master's acceptance of the gift of the Jeta Grove, she became a believer; and, later on, convinced by the preaching of an Arahant brother, she grew anxious in mind, entered the Order, strove and struggled for insight, and soon won Arahantship.

Thereafter, in consequence of her vow, she accumulated skill in the heavenly sight, and was assigned foremost place therein by the Master. And reflecting thereon, thrilled with gladness, she exulted thus:

While yet I dwelt as matron in the house,
I heard a Brother setting forth the Norm.
I SAW that Norm, the Pure, the Passionless,

Track to Nibbana, past decease and birth. (97)

Thereat I left my daughter, left my son,
I left my treasures and my stores of grain;
I called for robes and razors, cut my hair,
And gat me forth into the homeless life. (98)

And first as novice, virtuous and keen
To cultivate the upward mounting Way,
I cast out lust and with it all ill-will,
And therewith, one by one, the deadly Drugs.[217] (99)
Then to the Bhikkhunī of ripening power
Rose in a vision mem'ries of the past.[218]
Limpid and clear the mystic vistas grew,
Expanding by persistent exercise. (100)
Act, speech and thought I saw as not myself,[219]
Children of cause, fleeting, impermanent.
And now, with every poisonous Drug cast out,
Cool and serene I see Nibbana's peace. (101)

XLV
Soṇā. [220]

She, too, was born at the time when Padumuttara was Buddha, at Haŋsavatī, in a clansman's family. One day she sat listening to the Master, and hearing him place a Bhikkhunī at the top of those distinguished for capacity of effort, she vowed that this rank should one day be hers. And after many happy rebirths, she came to being, when this Buddha lived, in a clansman's family at Sāvatthī. She became, when married, the mother of ten sons and daughters, and was known as 'the Many-offspringed.' When her husband renounced the world, she set her sons and daughters over the household, handing over all her fortune to her sons, and keeping nothing for herself. Her sons and daughters-in-law had not long supported her before they ceased to show her respect. And saying, 'What have I to do with living in a house where no regard is shown me?' she entered the Order of Bhikkhunīs. Then she thought: 'I have left the world in my old age; I must work strenuously.' So, while she waited on the Bhikkhunīs, she resolved also to give herself religious studies all night. And she studied thus, steadfast and unfaltering, as one might cling doggedly to a pillar on the veranda, or to a tree in the dark, for fear of hitting one's head against obstacles, never letting go. Thereupon her strenuous energy became known, and the Master, seeing her knowledge maturing, sent forth glory, and appearing as if seated before her, said thus:

'The man who, living for an hundred years,
Beholdeth never the Ambrosial Path,
Had better live no longer than one day,
So he behold within that day, that Path!'[221]

And when he had thus spoken, she attained Arahantship. Now, the Exalted One, in assigning rank of merit to the Bhikkhunīs, placed her first for capacity of effort. One day, pondering hereon, she exulted thus:

Ten sons and daughters did I bear within
This heap of visible decay. Then weak
And old I drew near to a Bhhikkunī. (102)
She taught to me the Norm,[222] wherein I learnt
The factors, organs, bases of this self,
Impermanent compound. Hearing her words,
And cutting off my hair, I left the world. (103)
Then as I grappled with the threefold course, [223]
Clear shone for me the Eye Celestial.
I know the 'how' and 'when' I came to birth
Down the long past, and where it was I lived. (104)

I cultivate the Signless,[224] and my mind
In uttermost composure concentrate.
Mine is the ecstasy of freedom won
As Path merges in Fruit, and Fruit in Path. [225]
Holding to nought, I in Nibbana live. (105)
This five-grouped being have I understood.
Cut from its root, all onward growth is stayed.
I too am stayed, victor on basis sure,
Immovable.[226] Rebirth comes never more. (106)

XLVI
Bhaddā Kuṇḍalakesā, the ex-Jain. [227]

She, too, was reborn, when Padumuttara was Buddha, at Haŋsavatī, in a clansman's family. One day she sat listening to the Master, and hearing him place a Bhikkhunī at top of those whose intuition was swift, she vowed that this rank should one day be hers. After working much merit, and experiencing æons of rebirth among gods and men, she became, when Kassapa was Buddha, one of the seven daughters [228] of Kiki, King of Kāsī. And for twenty thousand years [229] she kept the precepts, and built a cell for the Order. Finally, in this Buddha-era, she was born at Rājagaha, in the family of the king's treasurer, and called Bhaddā. [230]Growing up surrounded by attendants, she saw, looking through her lattice, Satthuka, the chaplain's son, a highwayman, being led to execution by the city guard by order of the king. Falling in love with him, she fell prone on her couch, saying: 'If I get him, I shall live; if not, I shall die.' Then her father, hearing of her state, out of his great love for her, bribed the guard heavily to release the thief, let him be bathed with perfumed water, adorned him, and let him come where Bhaddā, decked in jewels, waited upon him. Then Satthuka very soon coveted her jewels, and said: 'Bhaddā, when the city guards were taking me to the Robbers' Cliff, I vowed to the Cliff deity that if my life were spared I would bring an offering. Do you make one ready.' Wishing to please him, she did BO, and adorning herself with all her jewels, mounted a chariot with him, and drove to the Cliff. And Satthuka, to have her in his power, stopped the attendants; and taking the offering, went up alone with her, but spoke no word of affection to her. And by his behaviour she discerned his plot. Then he bade her take off her outer robe and wrap in it the jewels she was wearing. She asked him what had she done amiss, and he answered: 'You fool, do you fancy I have come here to make offering? I have come to get your ornaments.' 'But whose, then, dear one, are the ornaments, and whose am I?' 'I know nothing of that division.' 'So be it, dear; but grant me this one wish: let me, while wearing my jewels, embrace you.' He consented, saying: 'Very well.' She thereupon embraced him in front, and then, as if embracing him from the back, pushed him over the precipice. And the deity dwelling on the mountain saw her do this feat and praised her cleverness, saying:

> Not in every case is Man tho wiser ever;
> Woman, too, when swift to see, may prove as clever.
> Not in every case is Man the wiser reckoned;
> Woman, too, is clever, an she think but a second.'

Thereafter Bhaddā thought: 'I cannot, in this course of events, go home; I will go hence, and leave the world.' So she entered the Order of the Nigaṇṭhas. [231]And they asked her: 'In what grade do you make renunciation?' 'In whatever is your extreme grade,' she replied, 'perform that on me.' So they tore out her hair with a palmyra comb. (When the hair grew again in close curls they called her Curlyhair.) During her probation she learnt their course of doctrine and concluded that: 'So far as they go they know, but beyond that there is nothing distinctive in their teaching.' So she left them, and going wherever there were learned persons, she learnt their methods of knowledge till, when she found none equal to debate with her, she made a heap of sand at the gate of some village or town, and in it set up the branch of a rose-apple, and told children to watch near it, saying: 'Whoever is able to join issue with me in debate, let him trample on this bough.' Then she went to her dwelling, and if after a week the bough still stood, she took it and departed.

Now at that time our Exalted One, rolling the wheel of the excellent doctrine, came and dwelt in the Jeta Wood near Sāvatthī, just when Curlyhair had set up her bough at the gate of that city.

Then the venerable Captain of the Norm [232] entered the city alone, and, seeing her bough, felt the wish to tame her. And he asked the children: 'Why is this bough stuck up here?' They told him. The Elder said: 'If that is so, trample on the bough.' And the children did so. Then Curlyhair, after seeking her meal in the town, came out and saw the trampled bough, and asked who had done it. When she heard it was the Elder, she thought, 'An unsupported debate is not effective,' and going back into Sāvatthī, she walked from street to street, saying: 'Would ye see a debate between the Sākyan recluses and myself?' Thus, with a great following, she went up to the Captain of the Norm, who was seated beneath a tree, and, after friendly greeting, asked: 'Was it by your orders that my rose-apple bough was trampled on?' 'Yes, by my orders.' 'That being so, let us have a debate together.' 'Let us, Bhaddā.' 'Which shall put questions, which shall answer?' 'Questions put to me; do you ask anything you yourself think of.' They proceeded thus, the Elder answering everything, till she, unable to think of further questions, became silent. Then the Elder said: 'You have asked much; I, too, will ask, but only this question.' 'Ask it, lord.' 'One–what is that?' [233] Curlyhair, seeing neither end nor point to this, was as one gone into the dark, and said: 'I know not, lord.' Then he, saying, 'You know not even thus much. How should you know aught else?'

taught her the Norm. She fell at his feet, saying: 'Lord, I take refuge with you.' 'Come not to me, Bhaddā, for refuge; go for refuge to the Exalted One, supreme among men and gods.' 'I will do so, lord,' she said; and that evening, going to the Master at the hour of his teaching the Norm, and worshipping him she stood on one side. The Master, discerning the maturity of her knowledge, said:

> 'Better than a thousand verses, where no profit wings the word,
> Is a solitary stanza bringing calm and peace when heard.'[234]

THE SUMMIT OF VULTURE PEAK.

And when he had spoken, she attained Arahantship, together with thorough grasp of the letter and the spirit. Now she entered the Order as an Arahant, the Master himself admitting her. And going to the Sisters' quarters, she abode in the bliss of fruition and Nibbana, and exulted in her attainment thus:

> Hairless, dirt-laden and half-clad[235] –so fared

I formerly, deeming that harmless things
Held harm, nor was I 'ware of harm
In many things wherein, in sooth, harm lay. (107)
Then forth I went from siesta in the shade
Up to the Vulture's Peak, [236]and there I saw
The Buddha, the Immaculate, begirt
And followed by the Bhikkhu-company. (108)
Low on my knees I worshipped, with both hands
Adoring. 'Come, Bhaddā!' the Master said!
Thereby to me was ordination given. [237](109)
Lo! fifty years have I a pilgrim been,
In Anga, Magadha and in Vajjī,
In Kāsī and the land of Kosala,
Nought owing, living on the people's alms. [238](110)
And great the merit by that layman gained,
Sagacious man, who gave Bhaddā a robe–
Bhaddā who now (captive once more to gear)
Is wholly free from bondage of the mind. (111)

XLVII
Paṭācārā.

She, too, was reborn, when Padumuttara was Buddha, at Haŋsavatī, in a clansman's family. One day she sat listening to the Master, and hearing him place a Bhikkhunī at top of those who were versed in the rules of the Order, she vowed that this rank should one day be hers. After doing good all her life, and being reborn in heaven and on earth, she gained rebirth, in the time when Kassapa was Buddha, as one of the seven Sisters, daughters of Kiki, King of Kāsī. [239]And for 20,000 years she lived a life of righteousness, and built a cell for the Order. While no Buddha lived on earth she dwelt in glory among the gods, and finally, in this Buddha-era, was reborn in the Treasurer's house at Sāvatthī. Grown up, she formed an intimacy with one of the serving-men of her house. When the parents fixed a day on which to give her hand to a youth of her own rank, she took a handful of baggage, and with her lover left the town by the chief gate and dwelt in a hamlet. When the time for her confinement was near, she said: 'Here there's none to take care of me; let us go home, husband.' And he procrastinated, saying: 'We'll go to-day; we'll go to-morrow' till she said: 'The foolish fellow will never take me there'; and setting her affairs in order while he was out, she told her neighbours to say she had gone home, and set forth alone. When he came back and was told this, he exclaimed: 'Through my doing a lady of rank is without protection,' and hurrying after her, overtook her. Midway the pains of birth came upon her, and after she was recovered, they turned back again to the hamlet. At the advent of a second child things happened just as before, with this difference: when midway the winds born of Karma blew upon her, [240]a great storm broke over them, and she said, 'Husband, find me a place out of the rain!' While he was cutting grass and sticks in the jungle, he cut a stake from a tree standing in an ant-hill. And a snake came from the ant-hill and bit him, so that he fell there and died. She, in great misery, and looking for his coming, while the two babies cried at the wind and the rain, placed them in her bosom, and, prone over them on the ground, spent the night thus. At dawn, bearing one babe at her breast, and saying to the other, 'Come, dear, father has left thee,' she went and found him seated, dead, near the ant-heap. 'Oh!' she cried, 'through me my husband is dead,' and wept and lamented all the night. Now, from the rain, the river that lay across her path was swollen knee-deep, and she, being distraught and weak, could not cross the water with both babies. So she left the elder on the hither side, and crossed over with the other. Then she spread out a branch she had broken off, and laid the babe on her rolled headcloth. But she was loth to leave the little creature, and turned round again and again to see him as she went down to the river. Now, when she was half-way over, a hawk in the air took the babe for a piece of flesh, and though the mother, seeing him, clapped her hands, shouting, 'Soo! soo!' the hawk minded her not, because she was far from him, and caught the child up into the air. Then the elder, thinking the mother was shouting because of him, got flustered, and fell into the river; so she lost both, and came weeping to Sāvatthī. And, meeting a man, she asked him: 'Where do you dwell?' And he said: 'At Sāvatthī, dame.' 'There is at Sāvatthī such and such a family in such and such a street. Know you them, friend?' 'I know them, dame; but ask not of them; ask somewhat else.' 'I am not concerned with aught else. 'Tis about them I ask, friend.' 'Dame, can you not take on yourself to tell? You saw how the god rained all last night?' 'I saw that, friend. On me he rained all night long. Why, I will tell you presently. But first, do you tell me of how it goes with that Treasurer's family.' 'Dame, last night the house broke down and fell upon them, and they burn the Treasurer, his wife, and his son on one pyre. Dame, the smoke of it can be seen.' Thereat grief maddened her, so that she was not aware even of her clothing slipping off. Wailing in her woe–

> 'My children both are gone, and in the bush
> Dead lies my husband; on one funeral bier
> My mother, father, and my brother burn,'

she wandered around from that day forth in circles, and because her skirt-cloth fell from her she was given the name 'Cloak-walker.'[241] And people, seeing her, said: 'Go, little mad-woman!' And some threw refuse at her head, some sprinkled dust, some pelted her with clods. The Master, seated in the Jeta Grove, in the midst of a great company, teaching the Dhamma, saw her wandering thus round and round, and contemplated the maturity of her knowledge. When she came towards the Vihāra he also walked that way. The congregation, seeing her, said: 'Suffer not that little lunatic to come hither.' The Exalted One said: 'Forbid her not,' and standing near as she came round again, he said to her: 'Sister, recover thou presence of mind.'[242] She, by the sheer potency of the Buddha regaining presence of mind, discerned her undressed plight, and shame and conscience arising, she fell crouching to earth. A man threw her his outer robe, and she put it round her, and drawing near to the Master worshipped at his feet, saying: 'Lord, help me. One of my children a hawk hath taken, one is borne away by water; in the jungle my husband lies dead; my parents and my brother, killed by the overthrown house, burn on one pyre.' So she told him why she grieved. The Master made her see, thus: 'Paṭācārā, think not thou art come to one able to become a help to thee. Just as now thou art shedding tears because of the death of children and the rest, so hast thou, in the unending round of life, been shedding tears, because of the death of children and the rest, more abundant than the waters of the four oceans:

'Less are the waters of the oceans four
Than all the waste of waters shed in tears
By heart of man who mourneth touched by Ill.
Why waste thy life brooding in bitter woe?'

Thus, through the Master's words touching the way where no salvation lies, the grief in her became lighter to bear. Knowing this, he went on: 'O Paṭācārā, to one passing to another world no child nor other kin is able to be a shelter or a hiding-place or a refuge. Not here, even, can they be such. Therefore, let whoso is wise purify his own conduct, and accomplish the Path leading even to Nibbana.' Thus he taught her, and said:

'Sons are no shelter, nor father, nor any kinsfolk.
O'ertaken by death, for thee blood-bond is no refuge.
Discerning this truth, the wise man, well ordered by virtue,
Swiftly makes clear the road leading on to Nibbana.

When he had finished speaking, she was established in the fruit of a Stream-winner,[243] and asked for ordination. The Master led her to the Bhikkhunīs, and let her be admitted.

She, exercising herself to reach the higher paths, took water one day in a bowl, and washing her feet, poured away some of the water, which trickled but a little way and disappeared. She poured more, and it went farther. And the third time the water went yet farther before it disappeared. Taking this as her basis of thought, she pondered: 'Even so do mortals die, either in childhood, or in middle age, or when old.' And the Master, seated in the 'Fragrant Chamber,' shed glory around, and appeared as if speaking before her, saying: 'Even so, O Paṭācārā, are all mortals liable to die; therefore is it better to have so lived as to see how the five khandhas come and go, even were it hut for one day–ay, but for one moment–than to live for a hundred years and not see that.

> 'The man who, living for an hundred years,
> Beholdeth never how things rise and fall,
> Had better live no longer than one day,
> So, in that day, he see the flux of things.'[244]

And when he had finished, Paṭācārā won Arahantship, together with thorough grasp of the Norm in letter and in spirit. Thereafter, reflecting on how she had attained while yet a student, and magnifying the advent of this upward change, she exulted thus:

> With ploughshares ploughing up the fields, with seed
> Sown in the breast of earth, men win their crops,
> Enjoy their gains and nourish wife and child. (112)
> Why cannot I, whose life is pure, who seek
> To do the Master's will, no sluggard am,

Nor puffèd up, win to Nibbana's bliss? (113)

One day, bathing my feet, I sit and watch
The water as it trickles down the slope.
Thereby I set my heart in steadfastness,
As one doth train a horse of noble breed. (114)
Then going to my cell, I take my lamp,
And seated on my couch I watch the flame. (115)
Grasping the pin, I pull the wick right down
Into the oil. . . .
Lo! the Nibbana of the little lamp!
Emancipation dawns! My heart is free! [245](116)

XLVIII
Thirty Sisters under Paṭācārā declare their AÑÑĀ.

They, too, having made vows under former Buddhas, and accumulating good of age-enduring efficacy in this and that rebirth, consolidated the conditions for emancipation. They came to birth, in this Buddha-dispensation, in clansmen's families in different places, heard Paṭācārā preach, and were by her converted, and entered the Order. To them, perfecting virtue and fulfilling their duties, she one day gave this exhortation: [246]

Men in their prime with pestle and with quern
Are busied pounding rice and grinding corn.
Men in their prime gather and heap up wealth,
To have and nourish wife and children dear. (117)
But ye, my sisters, see ye carry out
The Buddha's will, which bringeth no remorse.
Swiftly bathe ye your feet, then sit ye down
Apart; your souls surrender utterly
To spiritual calm–so do his will. (118)

Then those Bhikkhunīs, abiding in the Sister's admonition, established themselves in insight, performed exercises therein, and brought knowledge to such maturity–the promise, too, being in them–that they attained Arahantship, together with thorough grasp of the Norm in letter and in spirit. And reflecting thereon, they exulted thus, adding the Therī's verses to their own:

> The will of her who spake–Paṭācārā–[247]
> The thirty Sisters heard and swift obeyed.
> Bathing their feet, they sat them down apart,
> And gave their souls to spiritual calm,
> Fulfilling thus the bidding of the Lord. (119)
> While passed the first watch of the night, there rose
> Long memories of the bygone line of lives;
> While passed the second watch, the Heavenly Eye,
> Purview celestial, they clarified;
> While passed the last watch of the night, they burst
> And rent aside the gloom of ignorance. (120)
> Then rising to their feet they hailed her blest:
> 'Fulfillèd is thy will! and thee we take,
> And like to Sakka o'er the thrice ten gods,
> Chieftain unconquered in celestial wars,
> We place thee as our Chief, and so shall live.
> The threefold Wisdom have we gotten now.
> From deadly drugs our souls are purified.' (121)

XLIX
Candā.

She, too, faring in former ages like the foregoing, was, in this Buddha-era, born in a brahmin village as the daughter of a brahmin of whom nothing is known. From her childhood her family lost its possessions, and she grew up in wretched circumstances.

Now, in her home the snake-blast disease [248] broke out, and all her kinsfolk caught it, and died. She, being unable to support herself otherwise, went from house to house with a potsherd, maintaining herself by alms. One day she came to where Paṭācārā had just finished her meal. The Bhikkhunīs, seeing her wretched and overcome with hunger, received her with affectionate kindness in the pity they felt for her, and satisfied her with such food as they had. Gladdened by their virtuous conduct, she drew near to the Therī, saluted her, and sat down on one side while the Therī discoursed. She listened in delight, and, growing anxious concerning the round of life, renounced the world. Abiding in the Therī's admonition, she established insight, devoted to practice. Then, because of her resolve and of the maturity of her knowledge, she not long after won Arahantship, with thorough grasp of the Norm in the letter and the spirit. And, reflecting on her attainment, she exulted thus:

Fallen on evil days was I of yore.
No husband had I, nor no child, no friends
Or kin–whence could I food or raiment find? (122)
As beggars go, I took my bowl and staff,
And sought me alms, begging from house to house,
Sunburnt, frost-bitten, seven weary years. (123)
Then came I where a woman Mendicant [249]
Shared with me food, and drink, and welcomed me,
And said: 'Come forth into our homeless life!' (124)
In gracious pity did she let me come–
PAṬĀCĀRĀ–and heard me take the vows.
And thenceforth words of wisdom and of power
She spake, and set before my face
The way of going to the Crown of Life. [250](125)

I heard her and I marked, and did her will.
O wise and clear Our Lady's homily!
The Threefold Wisdom have I gotten now.
From deadly drugs my heart is purified. (126)

PSALMS OF SIX VERSES

L

Paṭācārā's Five Hundred. [251]

THESE too, having fared under former Buddhas as the foregoing Sisters, were, in this Buddha-era, reborn in some clansman's house in divers places, were married, and bore children, living domestic lives. And having wrought karma such as would bring to pass such a result, they suffered bereavement in the death of a child. Then they found their way, overwhelmed with grief, to Paṭācārā, and saluting her, and seated by, her, told her the manner of their sorrow. The Sister, restraining their sorrow, spake thus:

> The way by which men come we cannot know;
> Nor can we see the path by which they go.
> Why mournest then for him who came to thee,
> Lamenting through thy tears: 'My son! my son!' (127)
> Seeing thou knowest not the way he came,
> Nor yet the manner of his leaving thee?
> Weep not, for such is here the life of man. (128)
> Unask'd he came, unbidden went he hence.
> Lo! ask thyself again whence came thy son
> To bide on earth this little breathing space? (129)
> By one way come and by another gone,
> As man to die, and pass to other births–
> So hither and so hence–why would ye weep? [252](130)

They, hearing her doctrine, were filled with agitation, and, under the Therī, renounced the world. Exercising themselves henceforth in insight, their faculties growing ripe for emancipation, they soon became established in Arahantship, with thorough grasp of the Norm in form and in meaning. Thereafter, pondering on their attainment, they exulted in those words, 'The way by which men come,' adding thereto other verses, and repeating them in turn, as follows:

> Lo! from my heart the hidden shaft is gone,
> The shaft that nestled there she hath removed,
> And that consuming grief for my dead child
> Which poisoned all the life of me is dead. (131)
> To-day my heart is healed, my yearning stayed,
> Perfected the deliverance wrought in me. [253]
> Lo! I for refuge to the Buddha go–
> The only wise–the Order and the Norm. [254](132)

Now, because those 500 Bhikkhums were versed in the teaching of Paṭācārā, therefore they got the name of The Paṭācārā's.

LI
Vāsiṭṭhī. [255]

She, too, faring under former Buddhas like the foregoing, was, in this Buddha-era, reborn in a clansman's family at Vesālī. Her parents gave her in marriage to a clansman's son of equal rank, and she, bearing one son, lived happily with her husband. But when the child was able to run about, he died; and she was worn and maddened with grief. And while the relatives were administering healing to the husband, she, unknown to them, ran away raving, and wandered round and round till she came to Mithilā. There she saw the Exalted One going down the next street, self-controlled, self-contained, master of his faculties. And at the sight of the wondrous Chief, [256]and through the potency of the Buddha, she regained her normal mind from the frenzy that had befallen her. Then the Master taught her the

Norm in outline, and in agitation she asked him that she might enter the Order, and by his command she was admitted. Performing all requisite duties and preliminaries, she established insight, and, striving with might and main, and with ripening knowledge, she soon attained Arahantship, together with thorough grasp of the Norm in form and in spirit. Reflecting on her attainment, she exulted thus:

Now here, now there, lightheaded, crazed with grief,
Mourning my child, I wandered up and down,
Naked, unheeding, streaming hair unkempt, (133)
Lodging in scourings of the streets, and where
The dead lay still, and by the chariot-roads–
So three years long I fared, starving, athirst. (134)

And then at last I saw Him, as He went
Within that blessed city Mithilā:
Great Tamer of untamèd hearts, yea, Him,
The Very Buddha, Banisher of fear. (135)
Came back my heart to me, my errant mind;
Forthwith to Him I went low worshipping,
And there, e'en at His feet I heard the Norm.
For of His great compassion on us all,
'Twas He who taught me, even GOTAMA. [257](136)

I heeded all He said and left the world
And all its cares behind, and gave myself
To follow where He taught, and realize
Life in the Path to great good fortune bound. (137)
Now all my sorrows are hewn down, cast out,
Uprooted, brought to utter end,
In that I now can grasp and understand
The base on which my miseries were built. (138)

LII
Khemā.

Now she, when Padumuttara was Buddha, became a slave to others, dependent for her livelihood on others, at Haŋsavatī. And one day, seeing the Elder, Sujāta, seeking alms, she gave him three sweet cakes, and at the same time took down her hair [258] and gave it to the Elder, saying: 'May I in the future become a disciple, great in wisdom, of a Buddha!' After many fortunate rebirths as Queen among both gods and men, for that she had wrought good karma to the uttermost, she became a human, when Vipassi [259] was Buddha. Renouncing the world, she became a learned preacher of the Norm. Reborn, when Kakusandha was Buddha, in a wealthy family, she made a great park for the Order, and delivered it over to the Order with the Buddha at their head. She did this again when Koṇāgamana was Buddha. When Kassapa was Buddha she became the eldest daughter of King Kiki, [260]named Samaṇī, lived a pious life, and gave a cell to the Order. Finally, in this Buddha-era, she was born in Magadha, at Sāgala, [261]as one of the King's family, and named Khemā. Beautiful, and with skin like gold, she became the consort of King Bimbisāra. While the Master was at the Bamboo Grove[262] she, being infatuated with her own beauty, would not go to see him, fearing he would look on this as a fault in her. The King bade persons praise the Grove to her to induce her to visit it. And accordingly she asked him to let her see it. The King went to the Vihāra, and seeing no Master, but determined that she should not get away, he instructed his men to let the Queen see Him of the Ten Powers, even by constraining her. And this they did when the Queen was about to leave without meeting the Master. As they brought her reluctant, the Master, by mystic potency, conjured up a woman like a celestial nymph, who stood fanning him with a palmyra leaf. And Khemā, seeing her, thought: 'Verily the Exalted One has around him women as lovely as goddesses. I am not fit even to wait upon such. I am undone by my base and mistaken notions!' Then, as she looked, that woman, through the steadfast will of the Master, passed from youth to middle age and old age, till, with broken teeth, grey hair, and wrinkled skin, she fell to earth with her palm-leaf. Then Khemā, because of her ancient resolve, thought: 'Has such a body come to be a wreck like that? Then so will my body also!' And the Master, knowing her thoughts, said:

> 'They who are slaves to lust drift down the stream,
> Like to a spider gliding down the web
> He of himself has wrought. But the released,
> Who all their bonds have snapt in twain,
> With thoughts elsewhere intent, forsake the world,
> And all delight in sense put far away.' [263]

The Commentaries say that when he had finished, she attained Arahantship, together with thorough grasp of the Norm in form and meaning. But according to the Apadāna, she was established only in the Fruit of one who has entered the Stream, and, the King consenting, entered the Order ere she became an Arahant. [264]

Thereafter she became known for her great insight, and was ranked foremost herein by the Exalted One, seated in the conclave of Ariyans at the Jeta Grove Vihāra.

And as she sat one day in siesta under a tree, Māra the Evil One, in youthful shape, drew near, tempting her with sensuous ideas:

> Thou art fair, and life is young, beauteous Khemā! [265]
> I am young, even I, too–Come, O fairest lady!
> While in our ear fivefold harmonies murmur melodious,
> Seek we our pleasure.' (139)

'Through this body vile, foul seat of disease and corruption,
Loathing I feel, and oppression. Cravings of lust are uprooted. (140)
Lusts of the body and sense-mind [266] cut like daggers and javelins.
Speak not to me of delighting in aught of sensuous pleasure!
Verily all such vanities now no more may delight me. (141)
Slain on all sides is the love of the world, the flesh, and the devil. [267]
Rent asunder the gloom of ignorance once that beset me.
Know this, O Evil One! Destroyer, know thyself worsted! (142)

Lo! ye who blindly worship constellations of heaven,
Ye who fostering fire in cool grove, wait upon Agni,
Ignorant are ye all, ye foolish and young, of the Real,
Deeming ye thus might find purification from evil. [268](143)
Lo! as for me I worship th' Enlightened, the Uttermost Human, [269]
Utterly free from all sorrow, doer of Buddha's commandments.' (144)

LIII
Sujātā.

She, too, having made her resolve under former Buddhas, and accumulating good of age-enduring efficacy in this and that rebirth, and consolidating the essential conditions for emancipation, was, in this Buddha-era, reborn at Sāketa, in the Treasurer's family. Given by her parents in marriage to a

Treasurer's son of equal rank, she lived happily with him. Going one day to take part in an Astral Festival [270] in the pleasure-grounds, she was returning with her attendants to the town, when, in the Añjana Grove, she saw the Master, and her heart being drawn to him, she drew near, did obeisance, and seated herself. The Master, finishing his discourse in order, and knowing the sound state of her mind, expounded the Norm to her in an inspiring lesson. Thereat, because her intelligence was fully ripe, she, even as she sat, attained Arahantship, together with thorough grasp of the Norm in form and meaning. Saluting the Master, and going home, she obtained her husband's and her parents' consent, and by command of the Master was admitted to the Order of Bhikkhunīs. Reflecting on her attainment, she exulted thus:

Adorned in finery, in raiment fair,
In garlands wreathed, powdered with sandalwood,
Bedecked with all my jewelry, begirt (145)
With troop of handmaidens, and well-supplied
With food solid and soft, and drink enow,
From home I drove me to the fair pleasaunce. (146)
There did we sport and make a merry time,
Then gat us once more on the homeward way.
So entered we the grove called Añjana,
Hard by Sāketa, where amidst the trees
Stands the Vihāra [of the holy men]. (147)

Him saw I sitting there, Light of the World,
And went into his presence worshipping.
And of his great compassion for us all,
He taught to me the Norm–the One who Sees! (148)
Forthwith I, too, could pierce and penetrate,
Hearing the truth taught by the mighty Seer,
For there, e'en as I sat, my spirit touched [271]

The Norm Immaculate, th' Ambrosial Path. (149)

Then first it was I left the life of home,
When the blest Gospel [272] I had come to know,
And now the Threefold Wisdom have I won.
O wise and sure the bidding of the Lord! (150)

LIV
Anopamā.

She, too, having made resolve under former Buddhas, and heaping up good of age-enduring efficacy in this and that rebirth, perfecting the conditions tending to bring about emancipation, was, in this Buddha-era, reborn at Sāketa as the daughter of the Treasurer, Majjha. Because of her beauty she got the name 'Peerless' (An-opamā). When she grew up, many rich men's sons, Kings' ministers, and Princes, sent messengers to the father, saying: 'Give us your daughter Anopamā, and we will give this, or that.' Hearing of this, she–for that the promise of the highest was in her–thought: 'Profit to me in the life of the House there is none'; and sought the Master's presence. She heard him teach, and her intelligence maturing, the memory of that teaching, and the strenuous effort for insight she made, established her in the Third Path–that of No-return. Asking the Master for admission, she was by his order admitted among the Bhikkhunīs. And on the seventh day thereafter, she realized Arahantship. Reflecting thereon, she exulted:

Daughter of Treas'rer Majjha's famous house,
Rich, beautiful and prosperous, I was born
To vast possessions and to lofty rank. (151)
Nor lacked I suitors–many came and wooed;
The sons of Kings and merchant princes came
With costly gifts, all eager for my hand.
And messengers were sent from many a land

With promise to my father: 'Give to me (152)
Anopamā, and look! whate'er she weighs,
Anopamā thy daughter, I will give
Eightfold that weight in gold and gems of price.' (153)

But I had seen th' Enlightened, Chief o' the World,
The One Supreme. In lowliness I sat
And worshipped at his feet. He, Gotama, (154)
Out of his pity taught to me the Norm.
And seated even there I touched in heart
The Anāgāmi-Fruit, Third of the Paths,
And knew this world should see me ne'er return. (155)
Then cutting off the glory of my hair,
I entered on the homeless ways of life.
'Tis now the seventh night since first all sense
Of craving dried up within my heart. (156)

LV
Mahā-Pajāpatī the Gotamid.

Now she was born, when Padumuttara was Buddha, in the city of Haŋsavatī, in a clansman's family. Hearing the Master preaching, and assigning the foremost place for experience to a certain Bhikkhunī, she vowed such a place should one day be hers. Then, after many births, once more was she reborn in the Buddha-empty era, between Kassapa and our Buddha, at Benares, as the forewoman among 500 slave-girls. [273]Now, when the rains drew near, five Silent Buddhas came down from the Nandamūlaka mountain-cave to Isipatana, seeking alms; and those women got their husbands to erect five huts for the Buddhas during the three rainy months, and they provided them with all they required during that time. Reborn once more in a weaver's village near Benares, in the headman's family, she again ministered to Silent Buddhas. Finally, she was reborn, shortly before our Master came to us, at Devadaha, in the family of Mahā-Suppabuddha. [274]Her family name was Gotama, and she was the younger sister of the Great Māyā. And the interpreters of birthmarks declared that the children of both sisters would be Wheel-rolling Rulers.[275] Now, King Suddhodana, when he came of age, held a festival, and wedded both the sisters. After this, when our Master had arisen, and, in turning the excellent wheel of the Norm, came in course of fostering souls to Vesāli, his father, who had reached Arahantship, died.

Then the great Pajāpatī, wishing to leave the world, asked the Master for admission, but obtained it not. Then she cut off her hair, put on the robes, and at the end of the sermon now forming the Suttanta on strife and contention, she sallied forth, and together with 500 Sākya ladies whose husbands had renounced the world, went to Vesālī, and asked the Master, through Ānanda the Thera, for ordination. This she then obtained, with the eight maxims for Bhikkhunīs.

Thus ordained, the Great Pajāpatī came and saluted the Master, and stood on one side. Then he taught her the Norm; and she, exercising herself and practising, soon after obtained Arahantship, accompanied by intuitive and analytical knowledge. The remaining 500 Bhikkhunīs, after Nandaka's homily, became endowed with the six branches of intuitive knowledge.

Now, one day, when the Master was seated in the conclave of Ariyans at the great Jeta Grove Vihāra, he assigned the foremost place in experience to Great Pajāpatī, the Gotamid. She, dwelling in the bliss of fruition and of Nibbana, testified her gratitude one day by declaring her AÑÑĀ before the Master, in praising his virtue, who had brought help where before there had been none:

Buddha the Wake, [276]the Hero, hail! all hail!

Supreme o'er every being that hath life,
Who from all ill and sorrow hast released
Me and so many, many stricken folk. [277](157)
Now have I understood how Ill doth come.
Craving, the Cause, in me is dried up.
Have I not trod, have I not touched the End
Of Ill–the Ariyan, the Eightfold Path? (158)

Oh! but 'tis long I've wandered down all time.
Living as mother, father, brother, son,
And as grandparent in the ages past–
Not knowing how and what things really are,
And never finding what I needed sore. (159)
But now mine eyes have seen th' Exalted One;
And now I know this living frame's the last,
And shattered is th' unending round of births.
No more Pajāpatī shall come to be! (160)

Behold the company who learn of him–
In happy concord of fraternity,
Of strenuous energy and resolute,
From strength to strength advancing toward the Goal–
The noblest homage this to Buddhas paid. [278](161)

Oh! surely for the good of countless lives
Did sister Māyā bring forth Gotama,
Dispeller of the burden of our ill,
Who lay o'erweighted with disease and death! (162)

LVI
Guttā.

She, too, having made her resolve under former Buddhas, and accumulating good of age-enduring efficacy in this and that rebirth, and consolidating the essential conditions for emancipation, was, in this Buddha-era, reborn at Sāvatthī, in a brahmin's family, and named Guttā. When adolescent, life in the house became repugnant to her, and she obtained her parents' consent to enter the Order under the Great Pajāpatī. Thereafter, though she practised with devotion, her heart long persisted in running after external interests, and this destroyed concentration. Then the Master, to encourage her, sent forth glory, and appeared near her, as if seated in the air, saying these words:

Bethink thee, Guttā, of that high reward [279]
For which thou wast content to lose thy world,
Renouncing hope of children, lure of wealth.
To that direct and consecrate the mind,
Nor give thyself to sway of truant thoughts. (163)
Deceivers ever are the thoughts of men,
Fain for the haunts where Māra finds his prey;
And running ever on from birth to birth,
To the dread circle bound–a witless world. (164)
But thou, O Sister, bound to other goals,
Thine is't to break those Fetters five: the lust
Of sense, ill-will, delusion of the Self,
The taint of rites and ritual, and doubt, (165)
That drag thee backward to the hither shore.
'Tis not for thee to come again to this! (166)
Get thee away from life-lust,[280] from conceit,
From ignorance, and from distraction's craze;
Sunder the bonds; so only shalt thou come
To utter end of Ill. Throw off the Chain (167)
Of birth and death–thou knowest what they mean.
So, free from craving, in this life on earth,
Thou shalt go on thy way calm and serene. (168)

And when the Master had made an end of that utterance, the Sister attained Arahantship, together with thorough grasp of the Norm in form and meaning. And exulting thereon, she uttered those lines in their order as spoken by the Exalted One, whence they came to be called the Therī's psalm.

LVII
Vijayā.

She, too, having made her resolve under former Buddhas, and heaping up good of age-enduring efficacy, was, in this Buddha-era, reborn at Rājagaha, in a certain clansman's family. When grown up she became the companion of Khemā, afterwards Therī, but then of the laity. Hearing that Khemā had renounced the world, she said: 'If she, as a King's consort, can leave the world, surely I can.' So to Khemā Therī she went, and the latter, discerning whereon her heart was set, taught her the Norm so as to agitate her mind concerning rebirth, and to make her seek comfort in the system. And so it came to pass; and the Therī ordained her. She, serving as was due, and studying as was due, grew in insight, and, the promise being in her, soon attained to Arahantship, together with thorough grasp of the Norm in form and meaning. And she, reflecting thereon, exulted thus:

Four[281] times, nay five, I sallied from my cell,
And roamed afield to find the peace of mind
I lacked, and governance of thoughts
I could not bring into captivity. (169)
Then to a Bhikkhunī [282] I came and asked
Full many a question of my doubts.
To me she taught the Norm: the elements, (170)
Organ and object in the life of sense, [283]
[And then the factors of the Nobler life:]
The Ariyan Truths, the Faculties, the Powers,

The Seven Features of Awakening,
The Eightfold Way, leading to utmost good. (171)
I heard her words, her bidding I obeyed.
While [284] passed the first watch of the night there rose
Long memories of the bygone line of lives. (172)
While passed the second watch, the Heavenly Eye,
Purview celestial, I clarified.
While passed the last watch of the night, I burst
And rent aside the gloom of ignorance. (173)
Then, letting joy and blissful ease of mind
Suffuse my body, seven days I sat,
Ere stretching out cramped limbs I rose again.
Was it not rent indeed, that muffling mist? [285](174)

PSALMS OF SEVEN VERSES

LVIII
Uttarā.

SHE, too, having made her resolve under former Buddhas, and heaping up good of age-enduring efficacy in this and that rebirth, so that in her the root of good (karma) was well planted, and the requisites for emancipation were well stored up, was, in this Buddha-era, reborn at Sāvatthī, in a certain clansman's family, and called Uttarā. Come to years of discretion, she heard Paṭācārā preach the Norm, became thereby a believer, entered the Order, and became an Arahant. And, reflecting on her attainment, she exulted thus:

'Men in their prime, with pestle and with quern
Are busied pounding rice and grinding corn.
Men in their prime gather and heap up wealth,
To have and nourish wife and children dear. [286](175)
Yours is the task to spend yourselves upon
The Buddha's will which bringeth no remorse.
Swiftly bathe ye your feet, then sit ye down (176)
Apart. Planting your minds in Steadfastness,
With concentrated effort well composed,
Ponder how what ye do, and say, and think,
Proceeds not from a Self, is not your Self.' [287] (177)
The will of her who spake–Paṭācārā–
I heard and marked and forthwith carried out.
Bathing my feet, I sat me down apart. (178)
While passed the first watch of the night there rose
Long memories of the bygone line of lives.

While passed the second watch, the Heavenly Eye,
Purview celestial, I clarified. (179)
While passed the third watch of the night, I burst
And rent aside the gloom of ignorance.

Now rich in Threefold Wisdom I arose:
'O Lady! verily thy will is done. (180)
And like to Sakka o'er the thrice ten gods,
Chieftain unconquered in celestial wars,
I place thee as my chief, and so shall live.
The Threefold Wisdom have I gotten now.
From deadly drugs my soul is purified.' (181)

Now this Sister, one day, when under Paṭācārā she had established herself in an exercise, went into her own dwelling, and seating herself cross-legged, thought: 'I will not break up this sitting until I have emancipated my heart from all dependence on the Āsavas.' Thus resolving, she incited her intellectual grasp, and gradually clarifying insight as she progressed along the Paths, she attained Arahantship, together with the power of intuition and thorough grasp of the Norm. Thus contemplating nineteen subjects [288] in succession, with the consciousness that 'Now have I done what herein I had to do,' she uttered in her happiness the verses given above, and stretched her limbs. And when the dawn arose, and night brightened into day, she sought the Therī's presence, and repeated her verses.

LIX
Cālā.

She, too, having made her resolve under former Buddhas, and heaping up good of age-enduring efficacy in subsequent rebirths, was, in this Buddha-era, reborn in Magadha, at the village of Nālaka, [289]the child of Surūpasārī, the Brahminee. And on her name-giving day they called her Cālā. [290]Her younger sister was Upacālā, and the youngest Sīsūpacālā, and all three were junior to their brother Sāriputta, Captain of the Norm. Now, when the three heard that their brother had left the world for the Order, they said: 'This can be no ordinary system, nor ordinary renunciation, if one like our brother have followed it!' And full of desire and longing, they too renounced the world, putting aside their weeping kinsfolk and attendants. Thereupon, with striving and endeavour, they attained Arahantship, and abode in the bliss of Nibbana.

Now, Cālā Bhikkhunī, after her round and her meal, entered one day the Dark Grove to take siesta. Then Māra came to stir up sensual desires in her. Is it not told in the Sutta?

Again, Cālā Bhikkhunī, after her round in Sāvatthi and her meal, entered one day the Pleasant Grove for siesta. And, going on down into the Dark Grove, she sat down under a tree. Then Māra came, and, wishing to upset the consistency of her religious life, asked her the questions in her Psalm. When she had expounded to him the virtues of the Master, and the guiding power of the Norm, she showed him how, by her own attained proficiency, he was exceeding his tether. Thereat Māra, dejected and melancholy, vanished. But she discoursed in exultation on what both of them had said, as follows:

Lo here! a Sister who the fivefold sense [291]
Of higher life hath trained and, self-possessed,
Herself well held in hand, hath made her way
Where lies the Holy Path, where dwells the Bliss
Of mastery over action, speech and thought. (182)

Māra.

Why now and whereto art thou seen thus garbed

And shaven like a nun, yet dost not join
Ascetics of some sect, and share their rites?
What, futile and infatuate, is thy quest? (183)

Cālā.

'Tis they that are without, caught in the net [292]
Of the vain shibboleths on which they lean–
'Tis they that have no knowledge of the Truth,
'Tis they that lack all competence therein. (184)

Lo! in the princely Sākiya clan is born
A Buddha, peerless 'mong the sons of men:
'Tis he hath shown the saving Truth to me
Which vain opinions doth overpass. (185)
Even the What and Why of ILL, and how
Ill comes, and how Ill may be overpassed,
E'en by the Ariyan, the Eightfold Path,
That leadeth to th' abating of all Ill. (186)
And I who heard his blessed words abide
Fain only and alway to do his will.
The Threefold Wisdom have I gotten now, [293]
And done the bidding of the Buddha blest. (187)
On every hand the love of sense is slain. [294]
And the thick gloom of ignorance is rent
In twain. Know this, thou Evil One, avaunt!
Here, O Destroyer! shalt thou not prevail. (188)

LX
Upacālā.

Her story has been told in the foregoing number. Like Cālā, she, too, as Arahant, exulted, after Māra had tempted her in vain, as follows:

Lo! here a Sister who the fivefold sense
Of higher life hath trained, with memory
And power of inward vision perfected,
And thus hath made her way into the Path
Of Holiness, by noble spirits trod. (189)

Māra.

Why lovest thou not birth?[295] since, being born,
Thou canst enjoy what life of sense doth bring.
Enjoy the sport of sense and take thy fill,
Lest thou too late with bitter pangs regret. [296](190)

Upacālā.

To one that's born death cometh soon or late,
And many perils at the hands of men:
Scathe, torture, loss of limb, [297]of liberty,
Nay, life. So Ill-ward bound is the born child. (191)
Lo! in the princely Sākiya clan is born
He who is Wholly Wake, Invincible.
'Tis he hath shown the saving Truth to me
By which the round of birth is overpassed, (192)
Even the What and Why of ILL, and how
Ill comes, and how Ill may be overpassed,
E'en by the Ariyan, the Eightfold Path,
That leadeth to th' abating of all Ill. (193)

And I who heard his blessed words, abide
Fain only and alway to do his will.
The Threefold Wisdom have I gotten now,
And done the bidding of the Buddha blest. (194)
On every hand the love of sense is slain.

And the thick gloom of ignorance is rent
In twain. Know this, thou Evil One, avaunt!
Here, O Destroyer! may'st thou not prevail. (195)

PSALM OF EIGHT VERSES

LXI
Sīsupacālā

HER story has been told in that of Cālā her sister–how she followed in her great brother's steps, entered the Order, and became an Arahant. Dwelling in the bliss of fruition, she reflected one day on her attainment, and having done all that was to be done, exulted in her happiness thus:

> Lo! here a Sister, in the Precepts sure,
> Well-guarded in the sixfold way of sense, [298]
> Who hath attainèd to that Holy Path,
> That ever-welling elixir of life. [299](196)

Māra.

> Now think upon the Three-and-Thirty Gods,
> And on the gods who rule in realm of Shades,
> On those who reign in heaven of Bliss, and on
> Those higher deities who live where life
> Yet flows by way of sense and of desire: [300]
> Think and thither aspire with longing heart,
> Where in past ages thou hast lived before. (197)

When the Therī heard, she said: 'Stop, Māra! the Kāmaloka of which you talk is, even as is the whole of the world, burning and blazing with the fires of lust, hate, and ignorance. 'Tis not there the discerning mind can find any charm.' And showing Māra how her mind was turned away from the world and from desires of sense, she upbraided him thus:

Ay, think upon [301] the Three-and-Thirty gods,
And on the gods who rule in realm of Shades;
On those who reign in heaven of Bliss, and on
Those higher deities who live where life
Yet flows by way of sense and of desire. (198)
Consider how time after time they go
From birth to death, and death to birth again,
Becoming this and then becoming that,
Ever beset by the recurring doom
Of hapless individuality,
Whence comes no merciful enfranchisement. (199)

On fire is all the world, is all in flames!
Ablaze is all the world, the heav'ns do quake! [302](200)
But that which quaketh not, that ever sure,
That priceless thing, unheeded by the world,
Even the Norm–that hath the Buddha taught
To me, therein my mind delighted dwells. (201)
And I who heard his blessed word abide
Fain only and alway to do his will.
The Threefold Wisdom have I gotten now,
And done the bidding of the Buddha blest. (202)
On every hand the love of sense is slain
And the thick gloom of ignorance is rent
In twain. Know this, O Evil One, avaunt!
Here, O Destroyer, shalt thou not prevail! (203)

PSALM OF NINE VERSES

LXII
Vaḍḍha's Mother

SHE, too, having made her resolve under former Buddhas, and heaping up good of age-enduring efficacy in this and that rebirth, till the preparation for achieving emancipation was gradually become perfect, was, in this Buddha-era, reborn at the town of Bhārukaccha, [303]in a clansman's family. When married, she bore one son, and he was given the name Vaḍḍha. From that time she was known as Vaḍḍha's mother. Hearing a Bhikkhu preach, she became a believer, and, handing her child over to her kin, she went to the Bhikkhunīs, and entered the Order. The rest, not told here, may be filled in from Brother Vaḍḍha's story told in the Psalms of the Elder Brethren (Ps. ccii.). Vaḍḍha, to see his mother, went alone into and through the Bhikkhunīs' quarters and she, saying, 'Why have you come in here alone?' admonished him as follows:

O nevermore, my Vaḍḍha, do thou stray
Into the jungle of this world's desires.
Child of my heart! come thou not back and forth
To share, reborn, in all the ills of life. (204)
True happiness, O Vaḍḍha mine, is theirs
Who, wise and freed from longing and from doubt,
Cool and serene, have tamed the craving will,
And dwell immune from all the deadly drugs. (205)
The Way that Sages such as these have trod–
Leading to that pure vision how they may
Make a sure end of Ill–do thou, dear lad,

Study and cause to grow [304] to thine own weal. (206)

And Vaḍḍha, thinking, 'My mother is surely established in Arahantship,' expressed himself thus:

Now in good hope and faith thou speakest thus,
O little mother! well I trow, for thee.
Dear mother mine, no jungle bars the way. (207)

Then the Therī replied, showing her work was done:

Ah, no! my Vaḍḍha, whatsoe'er I do,
Or say, or think, in things or great or small,
Not e'en the smallest growth of jungly vice [305]
Yet standeth in the onward way for me. (208)
For all the deadly poison-plants are killed
In me who meditate with strenuous zeal.
The Threefold Wisdom have I gotten now,
And all the Buddha's word have I fulfilled. (209)

The Brother, using her exhortation as a goad, and stimulated thereby, went to his Vihāra, and, seated in his wonted resting-place, so made insight to grow that he attained Arahantship. And reflecting in happiness on his attainment, he went to his mother, and declared his AÑÑĀ:

O splendid was the spur my mother used,
And no less merciful the chastisement
She gave to me, even the rune she spoke,
Fraught with its burden of sublimest good. [306](210)
I heard her words, I marked her counsel wise,
And thrilled with righteous awe as she called up
The vision of salvation to be won. (211)
And night and day I strove unweariedly
Until her admonitions bore their fruit,

And I could touch Nibbana's utter peace. (212)

PSALM OF ELEVEN VERSES

LXIII
Kisā-gotamī.

NOW she was born, when Padumuttara was Buddha, in the city of Haŋsavatī, in a clansman's family. And one day she heard the Master preach the Dhamma, and assign foremost rank to a Bhikkhunī with respect to the wearing of rough garments. She vowed that this rank should one day be hers. In this Buddha-era she was reborn at Sāvatthī, in a poor family. Gotamī was her name, and from the leanness of her body she was called Lean Gotamī. And she was disdainfully treated when married, and was called a nobody's daughter. But when she bore a son, they paid her honour. Then, when he was old enough to run about and play, he died, and she was distraught with grief. And, mindful of the change in folk's treatment of her since his birth, she thought: 'They will even try to take my child and expose him.' So, taking the corpse upon her hip, she went, crazy with sorrow, from door to door, saying: 'Give me medicine for my child!' And people said with con-tempt: 'Medicine! What's the use?' She understood them not. But one sagacious person thought: 'Her mind is upset with grief for her child. He of the Tenfold Power will know of some medicine for her.' And he said: 'Dear woman, go to the Very Buddha, and ask him for medicine to give your child.' She went to the Vihāra at the time when the Master taught the Doctrine, and said: 'Exalted One, give me medicine for my child!' The Master, seeing the promise in her, said: 'Go, enter the town, and at any house where yet no man hath died, thence bring a little mustard-seed.' ''Tis well, lord!' she said, with mind relieved; and, going to the first house in the town, said: 'Let me take a little mustard, that I may give medicine to my child. If in this house no man hath yet died, give me a little mustard.' 'Who may say how many have not died here?' 'With such mustard, then, I have nought to do.' So she went on to a second and a third house, until, by the might of the Buddha, her frenzy left her, her natural mind was restored, and she thought: 'Even this will be the order of things in the whole town. The Exalted One foresaw this out of his pity for my good.' And, thrilled at the thought, she left the town and laid her child in the charnel-field, saying:

'No village law [307] is this, no city law,
No law for this clan, or for that alone;
For the whole world–ay, and the gods in heav'n–
This is the Law: ALL IS IMPERMANENT!'

So saying, she went to the Master. And he said: 'Gotamī, hast thou gotten the little mustard?' And she said: 'Wrought is the work, lord, of the little mustard. Give thou me confirmation.' Then the Master spoke thus:

'To him whose heart on children and on goods [308]
Is centered, cleaving to them in his thoughts,
Death cometh like a great flood in the night,
Bearing away the village in its sleep.' [309]

When he had spoken, she was confirmed in the fruition of the First (the Stream - entry) Path, and asked for ordination. He consented, and she, thrice saluting by the right, [310]went to the Bhikkhunīs, and was ordained. And not long afterwards, studying the causes of things, she caused her insight to grow. Then the Master said a Glory-verse: [311]

'The man who, living for an hundred years,
Beholdeth never the Ambrosial Path,
Had better live no longer than one day,
So he behold within that day the Path.'[312]

When he had finished, she attained Arahantship. And becoming pre-eminent in ascetic habits, she was wont to wear raiment of triple roughness. Then the Master, seated in the Jeta Grove in conclave, and assigning rank of merit to the Bhikkhunīs, proclaimed her first among the wearers of rough raiment. And she, reflecting on what great things she had won, uttered this Psalm before the Master, in praise of friendship with the elect:

Friendship with noble souls throughout the world
The Sage hath praised.[313] A fool, in sooth, grows wise
If he but entertain a noble friend. (213)
Cleave to the men of worth! In them who cleave
Wisdom doth grow; and in that pious love
From all your sorrows shall ye be released. (214)

Mark Sorrow well; mark ye how it doth come,
And how it passes; mark the Eightfold Path
That endeth woe, the Four great Ariyan Truths. (215)
Woeful is woman's lot! hath he declared,
Tamer and Driver of the hearts of men:
Woeful when sharing home with hostile wives,
Woeful when giving birth in bitter pain,
Some seeking death, or e'er they suffer twice, (216)
Piercing the throat; the delicate poison take.
Woe too when mother-murdering embryo
Comes not to birth, and both alike find death. (217)

'Returning [314] home to give birth to my child,
I saw my husband in the jungle die.
Nor could I reach my kin ere travail came. (218)

My baby boys I lost, my husband too.
And when in misery I reached my home,
Lo! where together on a scanty pyre,
My mother, father, and my brother burn!' (219)

O wretched, ruined woman! all this weight
Of sorrows hast thou suffered, shed these tears
Through weary round of many thousand lives. (220)
I too have seen where, in the charnel-field,
Devourèd was my baby's tender flesh. [315]

Yet she, her people slain, herself outcast,
Her husband dead, hath thither come
Where death is not! (221)
Lo! I have gone
Up on the Ariyan, on the Eightfold Path
That goeth to the state ambrosial. [316]
Nibbana have I realized, and gazed
Into the Mirror of the holy Norm. (222)
I, even I, am healèd of my hurt,
Low is my burden laid, my task is done,
My heart is wholly set at liberty.
I, sister Kisā-gotamī, have uttered this! (223)

PSALM OF TWELVE VERSES

LXIV
Uppalavaṇṇā.

SHE, too, was born, when Padumuttara was Buddha, at the city Haŋsavatī, in a clansman's family. And, when grown up, she heard, with a great multitude, the Master teach, and assign a certain Bhikkhunī the chief place among those who had mystic potency.[317] And she gave great gifts for seven days to the Buddha and the Order, and aspired to that same rank. . . .

In this Buddha-age, she was reborn at Sāvatthī as the daughter of the Treasurer. And because her skin was of the colour of the heart [318] of the blue lotus, they called her Uppalavaṇṇā.[319] Now, when she was come of age, kings and commoners from the whole of India sent messengers to her father, saying: 'Give us your daughter.' Thereupon the Treasurer thought: 'I cannot possibly meet the wishes of all. I will devise a plan.' And, sending for his daughter, he said: 'Dear one, are you able to leave the world?' To her, because she was in her final stage of life, his words were as if oil a hundred times refined had anointed her head. Therefore she said: 'Dear father, I will renounce the world!' He, honouring her, brought her to the Bhikkhunīs' quarters, and let her be ordained.

A little while afterwards it became her turn for office in the house of the Sabbath.[320] And, lighting the lamp, she swept the room. Then taking the flame of the lamp as a visible sign, and contemplating it continually, she brought about Jhana by way of the Lambent Artifice,[321] and making that her stepping-stone, she attained Arahantship. With its fruition, intuition and grasp of the Norm were achieved, and she became especially versed in the mystic potency of transformation.[322]

And the Master, seated in conclave in the Jeta Grove, assigned her the foremost rank in the mystic powers. She, pondering the bliss of Jhana and of fruition, repeated one day certain verses. They had been uttered in anguish by a mother who had been living as her daughter's rival with him who later, when a Bhikkhu, became known as the Ganges-bank Elder,[323] and were a reflection on the harm, the vileness and corruption of sensual desires:

I.

'In enmity we lived, bound to one man,
Mother and daughter, both as rival wives!
O what a woeful plight, I found, was ours,
Unnatural offence! My hair stood up. (224)
Horror fell on me. Fie upon this life
Of sensual desire, impure and foul,
A jungle thick with thorny brake, wherein
We hapless pair, my girl and I, had strayed!' (225)

The evils in the life of sense, the strong
Sure refuge in renouncing all, she saw.
At Rājagaha went she forth [324] and left
The home to live the life where no home is. (226)

II.

Joyful and happy, she meditates on the distinction she has won:

How erst I lived I know, the Heavenly Eye,

Purview celestial, have I clarified;
Clear too the inward life that others lead;
Clear too I hear the sounds ineffable; (227)
Powers supernormal have I made mine own;
And won immunity from deadly Drugs.
These, the six higher knowledges are mine.
Accomplished is the bidding of the Lord. (228)

III.

She works a marvel before the Buddha with his consent, and records the same:

With chariot and horses four I came,
Made visible by supernormal power,
And worshipped, wonder working, at his feet,
The wondrous Buddha, Sovran of the world. (229)

IV.

She is disturbed by Māra in the Sāl-tree Grove, and rebukes him:

Māra

Thou [325] that art come where fragrant the trees stand crownèd with blossoms,
Standest alone [in the shade, maiden so [fair and] foolhardy,
None to companion thee–fearest thou not the wiles of seducers? (230)

She

Were there an hundred thousand seducers e'en such as thou art,
Ne'er would a hair of me stiffen or tremble–alone what canst thou do? (231)
Here though I stand, I can vanish and enter into thy body. [326]See! I stand 'twixt thine eyebrows, stand where thou canst not see me. (232)

For all my mind is wholly self-controlled,
And the four Paths to Potency are throughly learnt,
Yea, the six Higher Knowledges are mine.
Accomplished is the bidding of the Lord. (233)

Like [327] spears and jav'lins are the joys of sense,
That pierce and rend the mortal frames of us.
These that thou speak'st of as the joys of life–
Joys of that ilk to me are nothing worth. (234)
On every hand the love of pleasure yields,
And the thick gloom of ignorance is rent
In twain. Know this, O Evil One, avaunt!
Here, O Destroyer! shalt thou not prevail. (235)

NOTE.–Four gāthā's ascribed to this famous Sister are, in the Therigāthā, recorded without break. The Commentary breaks them up into four episodes. In the first, a merchant's wife at Sāvatthī, about to bear her first child in her husband's prolonged absence on business at Rājagaha, is turned out by his mother, who disbelieves the wife's fidelity. She seeking her husband, and delivered of a son at a wayside bungalow, another merchant carries off the babe in her absence, and adopts it. A robber-chief finds the distracted mother, and she bears him a daughter. This child she accidentally injures, and flees from the chief's wrath. Years after her son, yet a youth, weds both mother and daughter, ignorant of the kinship. The mother discovers the scar on her daughter's head, and identifies her rival as her own child.

PSALM OF SIXTEEN VERSES

LXV

Puṇṇā or Puṇṇikā. [328]

SHE, too, having made her resolve under former Buddhas, and heaping up good of age-enduring efficacy in this and that rebirth, was, when Vipassi was Buddha, reborn in a clansman's family. Come to years of discretion, because of the promise that was in her, she waxed anxious at the prospect of rebirth, and, going to the Bhikkhunīs, heard the Norm, believed, and entered the Order. Perfect in virtue, and learning the Three Pitakas, she became very learned in the Norm, and a teacher of it. The same destiny befell her under the five succeeding Buddhas–Sikhi, Vessabhu, Kakusandha, Koṇāgamana, and Kassapa. But because of her tendency to pride, she was unable to root out the defilements. [329]So it came to pass, through the karma of her pride, that, in this Buddha-era, she was reborn at Sāvatthī, in the household of Anāthapiṇḍika, the Treasurer, of a domestic slave. She became a Stream-entrant after hearing the discourse of the Lion's Roar. [330]Afterwards, when she had converted (lit. tamed) the baptist [331] brahmin, and so won her master's esteem that he made her a freed woman, she obtained his consent, as her guardian and head of her home, to enter the Order. And, practising insight, she in no long time won Arahantship, together with thorough grasp of the Norm in form and in meaning. Reflecting on her attainment, she uttered these verses in exultation:

Drawer of water, I down to the stream, [332]
Even in winter, went in fear of blows,

Harassed by fear of blame from mistresses. (236)

'What, brahmin, fearest thou that ever thus
Thou goest down into the river? Why
With shiv'ring limbs dost suffer bitter cold?' (237)

'Well know'st thou, damsel Puṇṇikā, why ask
One who by righteous karma thus annuls
Effect of evil karma? Who in youth, (238)
Or age ill deeds hath wrought, by baptism
Of water from that karma is released.' (239)

'Nay now, who, ignorant to the ignorant,
Hath told thee this: that water-baptism
From evil karma can avail to free? (240)
Why then the fishes [333] and the tortoises,
The frogs, the watersnakes, the crocodiles
And all that haunt the water straight to heaven (241)
Will go. Yea, all who evil karma work–
Butchers of sheep and swine, hunters of game,
Thieves, murderers–so they but splash themselves
With water, are from evil karma free! (242)
And if these streams could bear away what erst
Of evil thou hast wrought, they'd bear away
Thy merit too, leaving thee stripped and bare. (243)
That, dreading which, thou, brahmin, comest e'er
To bathe and shiver here, that, even that
Leave thou undone, and save thy skin from frost.' (244)

'Men who in error's ways had gone aside
Thou leadest now into the Ariyan Path.
Damsel, my bathing raiment give I thee.' (245)

'Keep thou thy raiment! Raiment seek I none.
If ill thou fearest, if thou like it not, (246)

Do thou no open, nor no hidden wrong.
But if thou shalt do evil, or hast done, (247)
Then is there no escape for thee from ill,
E'en tho' thou see it come, and flee away.
If thou fear ill, if ill delight thee not, (248)
Go thou and seek the Buddha and the Norm
And Order for thy refuge; learn of them
To keep the Precepts. Thus shalt thou find good.' (249)

'Lo! to the Buddha I for refuge go,
And to the Norm and Order. I will learn
Of them to take upon myself and keep
The Precepts; so shall I indeed find good. (250)

Once but a son of brahmins born was I,
To-day I stand brahmin in very deed.
The nobler Threefold Wisdom have I won,
Won the true Veda-lore, and graduate
Am I, from better Sacrament returned,
Cleansed by the inward spiritual bath.' [334] (251)

For the brahmin, established in the Refuges and the Precepts, when later he had heard the Master preach the Norm, became a believer and entered the Order. Using every effort, he not long after became Thrice-Wise, [335]and, reflecting on his state, exulted in those verses. And the Sister, repeating them of herself, they all became her Psalm.

PSALMS OF ABOUT TWENTY VERSES

LXVI
Ambapālī.

SHE, too, having made her resolve under former Buddhas, and heaping up good of age-enduring efficacy in this or that rebirth, entered the Order when Sikhi was Buddha. And one day, while yet a novice, she was walking in procession with Bhikkhunīs, doing homage at a shrine, when an Arahant Therī in front of her hastily spat in the court of the shrine. Coming after her, but not having noticed the Therī's action, she said in reproof: 'What prostitute has been spitting in this place?'

As a Bhikkhunī, observing the Precepts, she felt repugnance for rebirth by parentage, and set her mind intently on spontaneous re-generation. So in her last birth she came into being spontaneously at Vesālī, in the King's gardens, at the foot of a mango-tree. The gardener found her, and brought her to the city. She was known as the Mango-guardian's girl. And such was her beauty, grace, and charm that many young Princes strove with each other to possess her, till, in order to end their strife, and because the power of karma impelled them, they agreed to appoint her courtezan. Later on, out of faith in the Master, she built a Vihāra [336] in her own gardens, and handed it over to him and the Order. And when she had heard her own son, the Elder Vimala-Kondañña, preach the Norm, she worked for insight, and studying the law of impermanence as illustrated in her own ageing body, she uttered the following verses:

Glossy and black as the down of the bee my curls once clustered.
They with the waste of the years are liker to hempen or bark cloth.
Such and not otherwise runneth the rune, the word of the Soothsayer. [337](252)

Fragrant as casket of perfumes, as full of sweet blossoms the hair of me.
All with the waste of the years now rank as the odour of hare's fur.
Such and not otherwise runneth the rune, the word of the Soothsayer. (253)

Dense as a grove well planted, and comely with comb, pin, and parting.
All with the waste of the years dishevelled the fair plaits and fallen.
Such and not otherwise runneth the rune, the word of the Soothsayer. (254)

Glittered the swarthy plaits in head-dresses jewelled and golden.
All with the waste of the years broken, and shorn are the tresses.
Such and not otherwise runneth the rune, the word of the Soothsayer. (255)

Wrought as by sculptor's craft the brows of me shone, finely pencilled.
They with the waste of the years are seamèd with wrinkles, o'erhanging.
Such and not otherwise runneth the rune, the word of the Soothsayer. (256)

Flashing and brilliant as jewels, dark-blue and long-lidded the eyes of me.
They with the waste of the years spoilt utterly, radiant no longer.
Such and not otherwise runneth the rune, the word of the Soothsayer. (257)

Dainty and smooth the curve of the nostrils e'en as in children.
Now with the waste of the years searèd [338] the nose is and shrivelled.
Such and not otherwise runneth the rune, the word of the Soothsayer. (258)

Lovely the lines of my ears as the delicate work of the goldsmith. [339]
They with the waste of the years are seamèd with wrinkles and pendent.
Such and not otherwise runneth the rune, the word of the Soothsayer. (259)

Gleamed as I smiled my teeth like the opening buds of the plantain.
They with the waste of the years are broken and yellow as barley.
So and not otherwise runneth the rune, the word of the Soothsayer. (260)

Sweet was my voice as the bell of the cuckoo [340] through woodlands flitting.
Now with the waste of the years broken the music and halting.
So and not otherwise runneth the rune, the word of the Soothsayer. (261)

Softly glistened of yore as mother-of-pearl the throat of me.
Now with the waste of the years all wilted its beauty and twisted.
So and not otherwise runneth the rune, the word of the Soothsayer. (262)

Beauteous the arms of me once shone like twin pillars cylindrical.
They with the waste of the years hang feeble as withering branches. [341]
So and not otherwise runneth the rune, the word of the Soothsayer. (263)

Beauteous of yore were my soft hands with rings and gewgaws resplendent.
They with the waste of the years like roots are knotted and scabrous. [342]
So and not otherwise runneth the rune, the word of the Soothsayer. (264)

Full and lovely in contour rose of yore the small breasts of me.
They with the waste of the years droop shrunken as skins without water.
So and not otherwise runneth the rune, the word of the Soothsayer. (265)

Shone of yore this body as shield of gold well-polishèd.
Now with the waste of the years all covered with network of wrinkles.
So and not otherwise runneth the rune, the word of the Soothsayer. (266)

Like to the coils of a snake [343] the full beauty of yore of the thighs of me.
They with the waste of the years are even as stems of the bamboo.
So and not otherwise runneth the rune, the word of the Soothsayer. (267)

Beauteous to see were my ankles of yore, bedecked with gold bangles.
They with the waste of the years are shrunken as faggots of sesamum.
So and not otherwise runneth the rune, the word of the Soothsayer. (268)

Soft and lovely of yore as though filled out with down were the feet of me.
They with the waste of the years are cracked open and wizened with wrinkles.
So and not otherwise runneth the rune, the word of the Soothsayer. (269)

Such hath this body been. Now age-weary and weak and unsightly,
Home of manifold ills; old house whence the mortar is dropping.
So and not otherwise runneth the rune, the word of the Soothsayer. (270)

And inasmuch as the Therī, by the visible signs of impermanence in her own person, discerned impermanence in all phenomena of the three planes, and bearing that in mind, brought into relief the signs of Ill and of No-soul, she, making clear her insight in her Path-progress, attained Arahantship.

LXVII
Rohiṇī.

She, too, having made her resolve under former Buddhas, and heaping up good of age-enduring efficacy in this and that rebirth, was born, ninety-one æons ago, in the time of Vipassi Buddha, in a clansman's family. One day she saw the Exalted One seeking alms in the city of Bandhumatī, and filling his bowl with sweet cakes, she worshipped low at his feet in joy and gladness. And when, after many rebirths in heaven and on earth in consequence thereof, she had accumulated the conditions requisite for emancipation, she was, in this Buddha-era, reborn at Vesālī, in the house of a very prosperous brahmin, and named Rohiṇī. [344]Come to years of discretion, she went, while the Master was staying at Vesālī, to the Vihāra, and heard the doctrine. She became a 'Stream-entrant,' and teaching her parents the doctrine, and they accepting it, she gained their leave to enter the Order. Studying for insight, she not long after attained Arahantship, together with thorough grasp of the Norm in form and meaning.

And reflecting on a discussion she had had with her father while she had yet only entered the Stream, she uttered the substance of it as verses of exultation:

'"See the recluses!" dost thou ever say.
"See the recluses!" waking me from sleep.
Praise of recluses ever on thy tongue.
Say, damsel, hast a mind recluse to be? (271)
Thou givest these recluses as they come,
Abundant food and drink. Come, Rohiṇī. [345]
I ask, why are recluses dear to thee? (272)
Not fain to work are they, the lazy crew.
They make their living off what others give.

Cadging are they, and greedy of tit-bits–
I ask, why are recluses dear to thee?' (273)

Full many a day, dear father, hast thou asked
Touching recluses. Now will I proclaim
Their virtues and their wisdom and their work. (274)

Full fain of work are they, no sluggard crew.
The noblest work they do, they drive out lust
And hate. Hence are recluses dear to me. (275)

The three fell roots of evil they eject,
Making all pure within, leaving no smirch,
No stain. Hence are recluses dear to me. (276)

Their work [346] in action's pure, pure is their work
In speech, and pure no less than these their work
In thought. Hence are recluses dear to me. (277)

Immaculate as seashell or as pearl,
Of lustrous characters compact, without,
Within. [346]Hence are recluses dear to me. (278)

Learn'd and proficient in the Norm; elect,
And living by the Norm that they expound
And teach. Hence are recluses dear to me. (279)

Learn'd and proficient in the Norm; elect,
And living by the Doctrine; self-possessed,
Intent. Hence are recluses dear to me. (280)

Far and remote they wander, self-possessed;
Wise in their words and meek, they know the end
Of Ill. Hence are recluses dear to me. (281)

And when along the village street they go,
At naught they turn to look; incurious
They walk. Hence are recluses dear to me. (282)

They lay not up a treasure for the flesh,
Nor storehouse-jar nor crate. The Perfected
Their Quest. Hence are recluses dear to me. (283)

They clutch no coin; no gold their hand doth take,
Nor silver. For their needs sufficient yields
The day. [347]Hence are recluses dear to me. (284)

From many a clan and many a countryside
They join the Order, mutually bound
In love. Hence are recluses dear to me.' (285)

'Now truly for our weal, O Rohiṇī,
Wert thou a daughter born into this house!
Thy trust is in the Buddha and the Norm
And in the Order; keen thy piety. (286)
For well thou know'st this is the Field supreme
Where merit may be wrought. We too henceforth
Will minister ourselves to holy men.
For thereby shall accrue to our account
A record of oblations bounteous.' (287)

'If Ill thou fearest, if thou like it not,
Go thou and seek the Buddha and the Norm,
And Order for thy refuge; learn of them
And keep the Precepts. So shalt thou find weal.' [348]
(288)

'Lo! to the Buddha, I for refuge go
And to the Norm and Order. I will learn

Of them to take upon myself and keep
The Precepts. So shall I indeed find weal. (289)

Once but a son of brahmins born was I.
To-day I stand brahmin in very deed.
The nobler Threefold Wisdom have I won,
Won the true Veda-lore, and graduate
Am I from better Sacrament returned,
Cleansed by the inward spiritual bath.' [349] (290)

For the brahmin, established in the Refuges and the Precepts, when later on he became alarmed, renounced the world, and, developing insight, was established in Arahantship. Reflecting on his attainment, he exulted in that last verse.

LXVIII
Cāpā.

She, too, having made her resolve under former Buddhas, and heaping up good of age-enduring efficacy in this and that rebirth, till she had accumulated the sources of good, and matured the conditions for emancipation, was, in this Buddha-age, reborn in the Vankahāra country, at a certain village of trappers, as the daughter of the chief trapper, and named Cāpā. [350]And at that time Upaka, an ascetic, [351]met the Master as he was going to Benares, there to set rolling from his Bo-tree throne [352] the Wheel of the Norm, and asked him: 'You seem, my friend, in perfect health! Clear and pure is your complexion. Wherefore have you, friend, left the world? or who may your teacher be? or whose doctrine do you believe in?' And he was thus answered:

'All have I overcome. All things I know,
'Mid all things undefiled. Renouncing all,
In death of Craving wholly free. My own

The Deeper View. Whom should I name to thee?
For me no teacher lives. I stand alone
On earth, in heav'n rival to me there's none.

Now go I on seeking Benares town,
To start the Wheel, the gospel of the Norm,
To rouse and guide the nations blind and lost,
Striking Salvation's drum, Ambrosia's alarm.'

The ascetic, discerning the omniscience and great mission of the Master, was comforted in mind, and replied: 'Friend, may these things be! Thou art worthy [353] to be a conqueror, world without end!' Then, taking a by-road, he came to the Vankahāra country, and abode near the hamlet of the trappers, where the head trapper supplied his wants. One day the latter, setting off on a long hunt with sons and brothers, bade his daughter not neglect 'the Arahant' [354] in his absence. Now, she was of great beauty; and Upaka, seeking alms at her home, and captivated by her beauty, could not eat, but took his food home, and laid down fasting, vowing he would die should he not win Cāpā. After seven days the father returned, and, on inquiring for his 'Arahant,' heard he had not come again after the first day. The trapper sought him, and Upaka, moaning, and rolling over, confessed his plight. The trapper asked if he knew any craft, and he answered, 'No;' but offered to fetch their game and sell it. The trapper consented, and, giving him a coat, brought him to his own home, and gave him his daughter. In due time she had a son, whom they called Subhadda. [355]Cāpā, when the baby cried, sang to him: 'Upaka's boy, ascetic's boy, game-dealer's boy, don't cry, don't cry!' mocking her husband. And he said at length: 'Do not thou, Cāpā, fancy I have none to protect me. [356]I have a friend, even a conqueror eternal, and to him I will go.' She saw that he was vexed, and teased him again and again in the same way, till one day, in anger, he got ready to go. She said much, but vainly, to prevent him, and he set out westward. And the Exalted One was then at Sāvatthī in the Jeta Grove, and announced this to the brethren: 'He who to-day shall come asking, "Where is the Conqueror eternal?" send him to me.' And Upaka arrived, and, standing in the midst of the Vihāra, asked: 'Where is the Conqueror eternal?' So they brought him, and when he saw the Exalted One, he said: 'Dost know me, Exalted One?' 'Yea, I know. But thou, where hast thou spent the time?' 'In the Vankahāra country, lord.' 'Upaka, thou art now an old man; canst thou bear the religious life?' 'I will enter thereon, lord.' The Master bade a certain Bhikkhu, 'Come, do thou, Bhikkhu, ordain him.' And he thereafter exercising and training himself, was soon established in the Fruition of the Path-of-No-Return, and thereupon died, being reborn in the Aviha heavens. [357]At the moment of that rebirth he attained Arahantship.

Seven have thus attained it, as it has been said.

But Cāpā, sick at heart over his departure, delivered her boy to his grandfather, and, following in the way Upaka had gone, renounced the world at Sāvatthī, and attained Arahantship. And uniting Upaka's verses with her own, she thus exulted:

(Her husband speaks.)

'Once staff in hand homeless I fared and free.
Now but a trapper am I, sunken fast
In baneful bog of earthly lusts, yet fain
To come out on the yonder side. My wife (291)
Plays with her child and mocks my former state,
Deeming her charm yet holdeth me in thrall.
But I will cut the knot and roam again.' (292)

Cāpā.

'O be not angry with me, hero mine!
O thou great prophet, be not wroth with me!
For how may he who giveth place to wrath
Attain to holy life and purity?' (293)

'Nay, I'll go forth from Nāla. [358]Who would live
At Nāla now, where he who fain to lead
A life of righteousness sees holy men
Beguilèd by the beauty of a girl!' (294)

'O turn again, my dark-eyed lover, come
And take thy fill of Cāpā's love for thee,
And I, thy slave, will meet thy every wish,
And all my kinsfolk shall thy servants be.' (295)

'Nay, were a man desirous of thy love,
He well might glory didst thou promise him
A fourth of what thou temp'st me here withal!' (296)

'O dark-eyed love, am I not fair to see,
As the liana swaying in the woods,
As the pomegranate-tree in fullest bloom
Growing on hill-top, or the trumpet-flower
Drooping o'er mouth of island cavern? See, (297)
With crimson sandal-wood perfumed, I'll wear
Finest Benares robe for thee–O why,
O how wilt thou go far away from me?' (298)

'Ay! so the fowler seeketh to decoy
His bird. Parade thy charms e'en as thou wilt,
Ne'er shalt thou bind me to thee as of yore.' (299)

'And this child-blossom, O my husband, see
Thy gift to me–-now surely thou wilt not

Forsake her who hath borne a child to thee?' (300)

'Wise men forsake their children, wealth and kin,
Great heroes ever go forth from the world,
As elephants sever their bonds in twain.' (301)

'Then this thy child straightway with stick or axe
I'll batter on the ground–to save thyself
From mourning for thy son thou wilt not go!' (302)

'And if thou throw the child to jackals, wolves,
Or dogs, child-maker without ruth, e'en so
'Twill not avail to turn me back again!' (303)

'Why, then, go if thou must, and fare thee well.
But tell me to what village wilt thou go,
What town or burg or city is thy goal?' (304)

'In the past days we went in fellowship,
Deeming our shallow practice genuine.
Pilgrims we wandered–hamlet, city, town,
And capital–we tramped to each in turn.' (305)

'But the Exalted Buddha now doth preach,
Along the banks of the Nerañjarā, [359]
The Norm whereby all may be saved from ill.
To him I go; he now my guide shall be.' (306)

'Yea, go, and take my homage unto him
Who is the supreme Sovran of the World,
And making salutation by the right, [360]
Do thou from us to him make offering.' (307)

'Now meet and right is this, e'en as thou say'st,
That I in doing homage, speak for thee

To him, the Supreme Sovran of the World.
And making salutation by the right,
I'll render offering for thee and me.' (308)

So Kāla went to the Nerañjarā,
And saw the very Buddha on the bank,
Teaching the Way Ambrosial: of Ill, (309)
And of how Ill doth rise, and how Ill may
Be overpast, and of the way thereto,
Even the Ariyan, the Eightfold Path. (310)
Low at his feet the husband homage paid,
Saluted by the right and Cāpā's vows
Presented; then the world again renounced
For homeless life; the Threefold Wisdom won,
And brought to pass the bidding of the Lord. (311)

'But the Exalted Buddha now doth preach
Along the banks of the Neraŋjarā.

LXIX
Sundarī.

She too, having made her resolve under former Buddhas, and heaping up good of age-enduring efficacy in this and that rebirth, was reborn thirty-one æons ago, when Vessabhu was Buddha, in a clansman's family. One day she ministered to the Master with alms, and worshipped him, and he perceived her believing heart, and thanked her. After celestial and other happy rebirths, her knowledge having come to maturity, she was, in this Buddha-age, reborn at Benares as the daughter of Sujāta, a brahmin. Because of her perfect form they called her Sundarī (Beauty). When she grew up, her younger brother died. Her father, overmastered by grief, and going to and fro, met the Therī Vāsiṭṭhī [361] When she asked him what afflicted him, he answered as in the first two verses. Wishing to allay his grief, she spoke the next two verses, and told him of her own griefless state. The brahmin asked her: 'How, lady, did you become free from grief (a-sokā)?' The Therī told him of the Three Jewels, the Refuges. 'Where,' he asked, 'is the Master?' 'He is now at Mithilā.' So the brahmin drove in his carriage to Mithilā and sought audience of the Master. To him the Master taught the Norm; and he believed, and entered the Order, attaining Arahantship on the third day, after strenuous effort in establishing insight.

But the charioteer drove his chariot back to Benares, and told the brahminee what had taken place. When Sundarī heard of it, she asked her mother, saying: 'Mother, I too would leave the world.' The mother said: 'All the wealth in this house belongs to you. You are the heiress of this family. Take up your heritage and enjoy it. Go not forth.' But Sundarī said: 'Wealth is no use to me. Mother, I would leave the world;' and, bringing the mother to consent, she abandoned her great possessions like so much spittle, and entered the Order (at Benares). And studying and striving because of the promise in her and the maturity of her knowledge, she attained Arahantship, with thorough grasp of the Norm in form and meaning.

Dwelling thereafter in the ease of fruition and the bliss of Nibbana, she thought: 'I will utter a Lion's Roar [362] before the Master.' And asking permission of her teacher, she left Benares, accompanied by a great following of Bhikkhunīs, and in due course came to Sāvatthī, did obeisance to the Master, and stood on one side. Welcomed by him, she declared her AÑÑĀ by extolling her relation to him as the 'daughter of his mouth,' and so on. Thereupon all her kinsfolk, beginning with her mother, and their attendants, renounced the world. She, reflecting on her attainment, and using her father's utterances in her own Psalm, exulted as follows:

Sujāta.

Dame of the brahmins, thou too in the past–
Thou knowest–'twas thy little babes [363] Death robbed
And preyed upon; and thou all night, all day
Madest thy bitter wail. Vāsiṭṭhī, say! (312)
How comes it that to-day thou, who hast lost
So many–was it seven?–all thy sons,
No more dost mourn and weep so bitterly? (313)

Vāsiṭṭhī.

Nay, brahmin, many hundreds of our babes,
And of our kinsfolk many hundred more,
Have we in all the ages past and gone
Seen preyed upon by Death, both you and I. (314)
But I have learnt how from both Birth and Death
A way there is t' escape. Wherefore no more
I mourn, nor weep, nor make my bitter wail. (315)

Sujāta.

Wondrous in sooth, Vāsiṭṭhī, are the words
Thou speakest! Whose the doctrine thou hast learnt?
Whence thine authority for speech like this? (316)

Vāsiṭṭhī.

'Tis He, the Very Wake, the Buddha, He
Who late, hard by the town of Mithilā,
Did teach the Norm, brahmin, whereby
All that hath life may put off every ill. (317)
When I, O brahmin, when I heard the Arahant
Reveal the Doctrine of the Non-Substrate,[364]
Forthwith the Gospel sank into my heart,
And all my mother-grief fell off from me. (318)

Sujāta.

Then I too straight will go to Mithilā,
If haply the Exalted Buddha may
Me, even me, release from every ill. (319)

The brahmin went; he saw the Awaken'd One,
Th' Emancipated, Him in whom
No base is found for rebirth, and from Him,
The Seer, Him who hath passed beyond all ill, (320)
He heard the Norm: the Truth of Ill, and how
Ill comes, and how Ill may be overpassed,
E'en by the Ariyan, the Eightfold Path,
That leadeth to the abating of all Ill. [365](321)
Forthwith the Gospel sank into his heart.
He left the world, he chose the homeless life.
On the third night of contemplation rapt,
Sujāta touched and won the Threefold Lore. [366](322)

'Come, charioteer, now drive this chariot home!

Wish thy good mistress health, the brahminee,
And say: "'The brahmin hath renounced the world.
On the third night of contemplation rapt
Sujāta touched and won the Threefold Lore."' (323)

And so the driver took the car and purse
Of money home, and wished his mistress health,
And said: 'The brahmin hath renounced the world.
On the third night of contemplation rapt
Sujāta touched and won the Threefold Lore.' (324)

Sundarī's Mother.

For this that thou hast heard, O Charioteer,
And tellest: that the brahmin hath attained
The Threefold Lore, no half-gift give I thee. [367]
Take thou the chariot, take the horses both,
And take a thousand pieces for thy pains. (325)

'Let them remain thine own, O brahminee,
Horses and chariot and the thousand coins,
For I, too, have a mind to leave the world,
Near him of chiefest wisdom to abide.' (326)

'But thou, my Sundarī, now that thy father hath gone forth, [368]
Leaving his home, renouncing all his great estate–
Cattle and horses, elephants, jewels and rings–
Dost thou at least come to thine own! Thou art the heir
Of this thy family. Do thou enjoy thy wealth.' (327)

'Cattle and horses, elephants, jewels and rings–
Ay, all that goes to make this fair and broad estate
Hath he put far from him, my father dear,

And left the world, afflicted for his son.
I, too, afflicted at my brother's death,
I have a mind like him to leave the world.' (328)

'May this, then, thine intention, Sundarī,
Thy heart's desire, be crownèd with success!
The food from hand to mouth, [369]glean'd here and there,
The patchwork robe–these things accomplishèd
Will purify in other after-world
Whate'er has poisoned life for thee in this.'[370] (329)

Sundarī.

I've trained me, Lady, in the threefold course. [371]
Clear shines for me the Eye Celestial.
I know the how and when I came to be
Down the long past, and where it was I lived. (330)
To thee I owe it, O thou noble friend,
Thou loveliest of the Therī Sisterhood,
That I the Threefold Lore have gotten now,
And that the Buddha's will hath been obeyed. (331)
Give to me, Lady, thy consent, for I
Would go to Sāvatthī, so that I may
Utter my 'lion's roar,'—my 'Hail, all hail!'—
In presence of the Buddha, Lord and Chief. [372](332)

See, Sundarī, the Master fair in hue,
His countenance as fine gold, clear and bright,
Him who is All-enlightened, Buddha, Best,
Tamer of untamed, never tasting fear. (333)

And see, O Master, Sundarī, who comes
To tell thee of Emancipation won,
And of the right no more to he reborn.

Who hath herself from passion freed
Unyoked from bondage, loosened from the world.
Accomplished now is her appointed work,
And all that drugged her heart is purged away. [373](334)

Lo! from Benares I am come to thee–
I, Sundarī, thy pupil, at thy feet,
O mighty Hero, see me worship here. (335)
Thou art Buddha! thou art Master! and thine,
Thy daughter am I, issue of thy mouth,
Thou Very Brahmin! [374]even of thy word.
Accomplished now is my appointed task,
And all that drugged my heart is purged away. (336)

'Welcome to thee, thou gracious maiden! thence
For thee 'twas but a little way to come. [375]
For so they come who, victors over self,
Are fain to worship at the Master's feet,
Who also have themselves from passion freed,
Unyoked from bondage, loosened from the world,
Who have accomplished their appointed task,
And all that drugged their hearts have purged away.'
(337)

LXX
Subhā (The Goldsmith's Daughter)

She, too, having made her resolve under former Buddhas, and heaping up good of age-enduring efficacy, so that she had progressively planted the root of good and accumulated the conditions of emancipation, was, in this Buddha-era, reborn at Rājagaha as the daughter of a certain goldsmith. From the beauty of her person she was called Subhā. Come to years of discretion, she went one day, while the Master was at Rājagaha, and belief in him had come to her, and did obeisance, seating herself on one side. The Master, seeing the maturity of her moral faculties, and in accordance with her wish, taught her the Norm enshrined in the Four Truths. She was thereby established in the fruition of Stream-entry, which is in countless ways adorned. Later she realized the disadvantages of domestic life, and entered the Order under the Great Pajāpatī the Gotamid, devoting herself to the higher Paths. From time to time her relations invited her to return to the world, urging its charms. To them thus come one day, she set forth the danger in house-life and in the world, preaching the Norm in the twenty-four verses below, and dismissed them cured of their desire. She then strove for insight, purifying her faculties, till at length she won Arahantship. As Arahant she spoke thus:

A maiden I, all clad in white, once heard (338)
The Norm, and hearkened eager, earnestly,
So in me rose discernment of the Truths.
Thereat all worldly pleasures irked me sore,
For I could see the perils that beset
This reborn compound, 'personality,'
And to renounce it was my sole desire. (339)
So I forsook my world–my kinsfolk all,
My slaves, my hirelings, and my villages,
And the rich fields and meadows spread around,
Things fair and making for the joy of life–
All these I left, and sought the Sisterhood,
Turning my back upon no mean estate. (340)

Amiss were't now that I, who in full faith
Renounced that world, who well discerned the Truth,
Who, laying down what gold and silver bring,
Cherish no worldly wishes whatsoe'er,
Should, all undoing, come to you again! (341)
Silver and gold avail not to awake,[376]

Or soothe. Unmeet for consecrated lives, [377]
They are not Ariyan–not noble–wealth. (342)
Whereby greed is aroused and wantonness,
Infatuation and all fleshly lusts,
Whence cometh fear for loss and many a care:
Here is no ground for lasting steadfastness. (343)
Here men, heedless and maddened with desires,
Corrupt in mind, by one another let
And hindered, strive in general enmity. (344)
Death, bonds, and torture, ruin, grief; and woe
Await the slaves of sense, and dreadful doom. (345)
Why herewithal, my kinsmen–nay, my foes–
Why yoke me in your minds with sense-desires?
Know me as one who saw, and therefore fled,
The perils rising from the life of sense. (346)
Not gold nor money can avail to purge
The poison of the deadly Āsavas.
Ruthless and murderous are sense-desires;
Foemen of cruel spear and prison-bonds. (347)
Why herewithal, my kinsmen–nay, my foes–
Why yoke me in your minds with sense-desires?
Know me as her who fled the life of sense,
Shorn of her hair, wrapt in her yellow robe. (348)
The food from hand to mouth, [378]glean'd here and there,
The patchwork robe–these things are meet for me,
The base and groundwork of the homeless life. [379](349)

Great sages [380] spue forth all desires of sense,
Whether they be in heaven or on earth;
At peace they dwell, for they freeholders are,
For they have won unfluctuating bliss. (350)
Ne'er let me follow after worldly lusts,
Wherein no refuge is; for they are foes,

And murderers, and cruel blazing fires. [381](351)
Oh! but an incubus is here, the haunt
Of dread and fear of death, a thorny brake,
A greedy maw it is, a path impassable,
Mouth of a pit wherein we lose our wits, (352)
A horrid shape of doom impending–such
Are worldly lusts; uplifted heads of snakes.
Therein they that be fools find their delight–
The blinded, general, average, sensual man. (353)

For all the many souls, who thus befooled
Err ignorant in the marsh of worldly lusts,
Heed not that which can limit birth and death. (354)

Because of worldly lusts mankind is drawn
By woeful way to many a direful doom–
Where ev'ry step doth work its penalty. [382](355)

Breeders of enmity are worldly lusts,
Engendering remorse and vicious taints.
Flesh baits, to bind us to the world and death. (356)

Leading to madness, to hysteria,
To ferment of the mind, are worldly lusts,
Fell traps by Māra laid to ruin men. (357)

Endless the direful fruit of worldly lusts,
Surcharged with poison, sowing many ills,
Scanty and brief its sweetness, stirring strife,
And withering the brightness of our days. (358)

For me who thus have chosen, ne'er will I
Into the world's disasters come again,
For in Nibbana is my joy alway. (359)

So, fighting a [good] fight with worldly lusts,
I wait in hope for the Cool Blessedness,
Abiding earnest in endeavour, till
Nought doth survive that fetters me to them. (360)

THIS is my Way, the Way that leads past grief,
Past all that doth defile, the haven sure,
Even the Ariyan Eightfold Path, called Straight. [383]
There do I follow where the Saints [384] have crossed.
(361)

* * * * *

See now this Subhā, standing on the Norm,
Child of a craftsman in the art of gold!
Behold! she hath attained to utter calm;
Museth in rapture 'neath the spreading boughs. (362)
To-day, the eighth it is since she went forth
In faith, and radiant in the Gospel's light.
By Uppalavaṇṇā [385] instructed, lo!
Thrice wise is she and conqueror over death. (363)

Freed woman she, discharged is all her debt,
A Bhikkhunī, trained in the higher sense.
All sundered are the Bonds, her task is done,
And the great Drugs that poisoned her are purged. (364)

To her came Sakka, and his band of gods
In all their glory, worshipping Subhā,
Child of a craftsman in the art of gold,
But lord of all things that have life and breath. [386](365)

When, on the eighth day after her ordination, she won Arahantship, attaining fruition, seated beneath a tree, the

Exalted One uttered these three verses (362-364) in her praises, pointing her out to the Brethren. And the last verse was added by them who recited (the canon at the Council), to celebrate Sakka's adoration.

PSALM OF ABOUT THIRTY VERSES

LXXI
Subhā of Jīvaka's Mango-grove. [387]

SHE too, having made her resolve under former Buddhas, and heaping up good of age-enduring efficacy in this and that rebirth, fostering the root of good and perfecting the conditions for emancipation through the ripening of her knowledge, was in this Buddha-era reborn at Rājagaha, in the family of a very eminent brahmin. Her name was Subhā, and truly lovely was her body in all its members. It was for this reason that she came to be so called. While the Master sojourned at Rājagaha, she received faith and became a lay-disciple. Later she grew anxious over the round of life, and saw the bane of the pleasures of sense, and discerned that safety lay in renunciation. She entered the Order under the Great Pajāpatī the Gotamid, and exercising herself in insight, was soon established in the fruition of the Path of No-return.

Now one day a certain libertine of Rājagaha, in the prime of youth, was standing in the Jīvaka Mango-grove, and saw her going to siesta; and feeling enamoured, he barred her way, soliciting her to sensual pleasures. She declared to him by many instances the bane of sensuous pleasures and her own choice of renunciation, teaching him the Norm. Even then he was not cured, but persisted. The Therī, not stopping short at her own words, and seeing his passion for the beauty of her eyes, extracted one of them, and handed it to him, saying: 'Come, then! here is the offending eye of her!' Thereat the man was horrified and appalled and, his lust all gone, asked her forgiveness. The Therī went to the Master's presence, and there, at sight of Him, her eye became as it was before. Thereat she stood vibrating with unceasing joy at the Buddha. The Master, knowing the state of her mind, taught her, and showed her exercise for reaching the highest. Repressing her joy, she developed insight, and attained Arahantship, together with thorough grasp of the Norm in form and meaning. Thereafter, abiding in the bliss and fruition of Nibbana, she, reflecting on what she had won, uttered her dialogue with the libertine in these verses:

In Jīvaka's pleasant woodland walked Subhā
The Bhikkhunī. A gallant met her there
And barred the way. To him thus spake Subhā: [388](366)

'What have I done to offend thee, that thus in my path thou comest?
No man, O friend, it beseemeth to touch a Sister in Orders. (367)
So hath my Master ordained in the precepts we honour and follow;
So hath the Welcome One taught in the training wherein they have trained me,
Purified discipline holy. Why standest thou blocking my pathway? (368)
Me pure, thou impure of heart; me passionless, thou of vile passions;
Me who as to the whole of me freed am in spirit and blameless,
Me whence comes it that Thou dost hinder, standing obnoxious?' (369)

'Young art thou, maiden, and faultless–what seekest thou in the holy life?

Cast off that yellow-hued raiment and come! in the blossoming woodland
Seek we our pleasure. Filled with the incense of blossoms the trees waft (370)
Sweetness. See, the spring's at the prime, the season of happiness!
Come with me then to the flowering woodland, and seek we our pleasure. (371)
Sweet overhead is the sough of the blossoming crests of the forest
Swayed by the Wind-gods. But an thou goest alone in the jungle,
Lost in its depths, how wilt thou find aught to delight or content thee? (372)
Haunted is the great forest with many a herd of wild creatures,
Broken its peace by the tramplings of elephants rutting and savage.
Empty of mankind and fearsome [389] –is't there thou would'st go uncompanioned? (373)

Thou like a gold-wrought statue, like nymph in celestial garden
Movest, O peerless creature. Radiant would shine thy loveliness
Robed in raiment of beauty, diaphanous gear of Benares. (374)
I would live but to serve thee, an thou would'st abide in the woodland.
Dearer and sweeter to me than art thou in the world is no creature,
Thou with the languid and slow-moving eyes of an elf of the forest. (375)

If thou wilt list to me, come where the joys of the sheltered life [390] wait thee:
Dwell in a house of verandas and terraces, handmaidens serving thee. (376)
Robe thyself in delicate gear of Benares, don garlands, use unguents.
Ornaments many and divers I give to thee, fashioned with precious stones,
Gold work and pearls. And thou shalt mount on a couch fair and sumptuous, (377)
Carvèd in sandalwood, fragrant with essences, spread with new pillows,
Coverlets fleecy and soft, and decked with immaculate canopies. (378)
Like to a lotus upborne on the bosom of sprite-haunted water,
Thou, O chaste anchorite, farest to old age, thy beauty unmated.' (379)

'What now to thee, in this carrion-filled, grave-filling carcass so fragile
Seen by thee, seemeth to warrant the doctrine thou speakest, infatuate?' (380)

'Eyes hast thou like the gazelle's, like an elf's in the heart of the mountains–
'Tis those eyes of thee, sight of which feedeth the depth of my passion. (381)
Shrined in thy dazzling, immaculate face as in calyx of lotus,
'Tis those eyes of thee, sight of which feedeth the strength of my passion. (382)
Though thou be far from me, how could I ever forget thee, O maiden,

Thee of the long-drawn eyelashes, thee of the eyes so miraculous?
Dearer to me than those orbs is naught, O thou witching-eyed fairy!' (383)

'Lo! thou art wanting to walk where no path is; thou seekest to capture
Moon from the skies for thy play; thou would'st jump o'er the ridges of Meru, [391]
Thou who presumest to lie in wait for a child of the Buddha! (384)
Nowhere in earth or in heaven lives now any object of lust for me.
Him I know not. What like is he? Slain, root and branch, through the Noble Path. (385)
Hurled as live coal from the hand, and rated as deadly as poison-cup,
Him I see not. What like is he? Slain, root and branch, through the Noble Path. (386)
Tempt thou some woman who hath not discerned what I say, or whose teacher
Is but a learner; haply she'll listen; tempt thou not Subhā;
She understandeth. And now 'tis thyself hast vexation and failure. (387)
For I have set my mind to be watchful in whatso befalls me–
Blame or honour, gladness or sorrow–and knowing the principle:–
'Foul are all composite things,' nowhere the mind of me clings to them. (388)

Yea, the disciple am I of the Welcome One; onward the march of me

Riding the Car of the Road that is Eightfold. Drawn are the arrows
Out of my wounds, and purged is my spirit of drugging Intoxicants.
So I am come to haunts that are Empty. [392]There lies my pleasure. (389)

Oh! I have seen it–a puppet well painted, with new wooden spindles,
Cunningly fastened with strings and with pins, and diversely dancing. (390)
But if the strings and the pins be all drawn out and loosened and scattered,
So that the puppet be made non-existent and broken in pieces,
Which of the parts wilt thou choose and appoint for thy heart's rest and solace? (391)
Such is the manner wherein persist these poor little bodies:
Take away members and attributes–nothing surviveth in any wise.
Nothing surviveth! Which dost thou choose for thy heart's rest and solace? (392)
E'en as a fresco one sees drawn on a wall, painted in ochre,
[Giveth us naught of the true and the real, save in the seeming ;] [393]
Thou herein with vision perverted [canst not distinguish;
Judgest with] wisdom of average human, fallible, worthless. (393)
O thou art blind! thou chasest a sham, deluded by puppet shows
Seen in the midst of the crowd; thou deemest of value and genuine

Conjurer's trickwork, trees all of gold that we see in our dreaming. (394)
What is this eye but a little ball lodged in the fork of a hollow tree,
Bubble of film, anointed with tear-brine, exuding slime-drops,
Compost wrought in the shape of an eye of manifold aspects?' [394] (395)

Forthwith the maiden so lovely tore out her eye and gave it him:
'èHere, then! take thou thine eye!' Nor sinned she, her heart unobstructed. (396)
Straightway the lust in him ceasèd and he her pardon imploring:
'O that thou mightest recover thy sight, thou maid pure and holy!
Never again will I dare to offend thee after this fashion. (397)
Sore hast thou smitten my sin; blazing flames have I clasped to my bosom;
Poisonous snake have I handled–but O! be thou heal'd and forgive me!' (398)
Freed from molesting, the Bhikkhunī went on her way to the Buddha,
Chief of th' Awakened. There in his presence, seeing those features
Born of uttermost merit, straightway her sight was restored to her. (399)

'Sweet overhead is the sough of the blossoming crests of the forest Swayed by the wind-gods.

PSALM OF OVER FORTY VERSES[395]

LXXII
Isidāsī.

SHE too, having made her resolve under former Buddhas, and persisting in her former disposition in this and that rebirth, in that she heaped up good of age-enduring efficacy, in the seventh rebirth before her last phase of life, susceptible to sex-attraction, wrought adulterous conduct. For this she did purgatory for many centuries, and thereafter for three rebirths was an animal. Thereafter she was brought forth by a slave-woman as an hermaphrodite, and thereafter she was born as the daughter of a poor common man, and was, when of age, married to the son of a caravan-leader named Giridāsa. Now the wife that he had was virtuous and of noble qualities, and the new wife envied her, and quarrelled with the husband because of her. After her death she was, in this Buddha-era, reborn at Ujjenī [396] as the daughter of a virtuous, honoured and wealthy merchant, and was named Isidāsī. [397]When she was of age, her parents gave her in marriage to a merchant's son, a good match with herself. For a month she dwelt with him as a devoted wife; then, as the fruit of her previous actions, her husband became estranged from her, and turned her out of his house. All this is told in the Pali text. Because she had not proved desirable for one husband after another, she grew agitated and, gaining her father's consent, took orders under the Therī Jinadattā. And studying for insight, she not long after attained Arahantship, together with thorough grasp of the Norm in form and meaning.

Dwelling in the bliss of fruition and Nibbana, she one day, after seeking her meal in the city of Patna and dining, sat down on a sandbank of great Ganges, and being asked by her companion, the Therī Bodhi, about her previous experience, she related it by way of verses. And to show the connection of her former and latter replies, these three stanzas were inserted by the Recensionists:

In the fair city of Patna, earth's fairest city,
Named for its beauty after the Trumpet-flower, [398]
Dwelt two saintly Sisters, born of the Sākiyas, (400)
Isidāsī the one, Bodhi the other.
Precept-observers, lovers of Jhāna-rapture,
Learnèd ladies and cleansed from the taint of all worldliness. (401)
These having made their round, and broken their fast-ing,
Washed their bowls, and sitting in happy seclusion,
Spake thus one to the other, asking and answering: (402)

'Thou hast a lovely mien, Isidāsī,
Fresh and unwithered yet thy woman's prime,
What flaw in the life yonder hast thou seen,
That thou didst choose surrender for thy lot?' (403)
Then in that quiet spot Isidāsī,
Skilled in the exposition of the Norm,
Took up her tale and thus did make reply:
'Hear, Bodhi, how it was that I came forth. (404)

In Ujjenī, [399]Avantī's foremost town,
My father dwells, a virtuous citizen,
His only daughter I, his well-beloved,
The fondly cherished treasure of his life. (405)
Now from Sāketa came a citizen

Of the first rank and rich exceedingly
To ask my hand in marriage for his son.
And father gave me him, as daughter-in-law. (406)
My salutation morn and eve I brought
To both the parents of my husband, low
Bowing my head and kneeling at their feet,
According to the training given me. (407)
My husband's sisters and his brothers too,
And all his kin, scarce were they entered when
I rose in timid zeal and gave them place. (408)
And as to food, or boiled or dried, and drink,
That which was to be stored I set aside,
And served it out and gave to whom 'twas due. (409)
Rising betimes, I went about the house,
Then with my hands and feet well cleansed I went
To bring respectful greeting to my lord, (410)
And taking comb and mirror, unguents, soap,
I dressed and groomed him as a handmaid might. (411)
I boiled the rice, I washed the pots and pans;
And as a mother on her only child,
So did I minister to my good man. (412)
For me, who with toil infinite thus worked,
And rendered service with a humble mind,
Rose early, ever diligent and good,
For me he nothing felt save sore dislike. (413)
Nay, to his mother and his father he
Thus spake:–'Give ye me leave and I will go,
For not with Isidāsī will I live
Beneath one roof, nor ever dwell with her.' (414)

'O son, speak not on this wise of thy wife,
For wise is Isidāsī and discreet,
An early riser and a housewife diligent.
Say, doth she find no favour in thine eyes?' (415)

'In nothing doth she work me harm, and yet
With Isidāsī will I never live.
I cannot suffer her. Let be, let be!
Give ye me leave and I will go away.' (416)
And when they heard, mother and father-in-law
Asked of me: 'What then hast thou done t' offend?
Speak to us freely, child, and speak the truth.' (417)

'Naught have I done that could offend, nor harm,
Nor nagged at evil words. What can I do, [400]
That me my husband should so sore mislike?' (418)

To guard and keep their son, they took me back,
Unwilling guides, to father's house, distressed,
Distraught: 'Alas! we're beaten, pretty Luck!' [401] (419)

Then father gave me for the second time as bride,
Content with half my husband's sire had paid. (420)
From that house too, when I had dwelt a month,
I was sent back, though I had worked and served,
Blameless and virtuous, as any slave. (421)
And yet a third, a friar begging alms–
One who had self controlled, and could control
Favour in fellow-men–my father met
And spake him thus: 'Be thou my son-in-law!
Come, throw away that ragged robe and pot!' (422)
He came, and so we dwelt one half moon more
Together. Then to father thus he spake:
'O give me back my frock, my bowl and cup.
Let me away to seek once more my scraps.' (423)
Then to him father, mother, all the tribe
Of kinsfolk clamouring: 'What is it then
Here dwelling likes you not? Say quick, what is't
That we can do to make you better pleased?' (424)

Then he: 'If for myself I can suffice,
Enough for me. One thing I know:–beneath
One roof with Isidāsī I'll not live!' (425)

Dismissed he went. I too, alone I thought.
And then I asked my parents' leave to die,
Or, that they suffer me to leave the world. (426)
Now Lady Jinadattā on her beat
Came by my father's house for daily alms,
Mindful of every moral precept, she,
Learnèd and expert in the Vinaya. [402](427)
And seeing her we rose, and I prepared
A seat for her, and as she sat I knelt,
Then gave her food, both boiled and dried, (428)
And water–dishes we had set aside–
And satisfied her hunger. Then I said:
'Lady, I wish to leave the world.' 'Why here,' (429)
My father said, 'dear child, is scope for thee
To walk according to the Norm. With food
And drink canst gratify the holy folk
And the twice-born. [403]But of my father I, (430)
Weeping and holding out clasped hands, besought:
'Nay, but the evil karma I have done,
That would I expiate and wear away.'[404] (431)
Then father said: 'Win thou Enlightenment
And highest Truth, and gain Nibbana.
That Hath He, the Best of Beings, [405]realized.' (432)

Then to my mother and my father dear,
And all my kinsfolk tribe I bade farewell.
And only seven days had I gone forth
Ere I had touched and won the Threefold Lore. (433)
Then did I come to know my former births,
E'en seven thereof, and how e'en now I reap

The harvest, the result, that then I sowed.
That will I now declare to thee, an thou
Wilt listen single-minded to my tale. (434)

In Erakaccha's [406] town of yore I lived,
A wealthy craftsman in all works of gold.
Incensed by youth's hot blood, a wanton, I
Assailed the virtue of my neighbours' wives. (435)
Therefrom deceasing, long I cooked [407] in hell,
Till, fully ripened, I emerged, and then
Found rebirth in the body of an ape. (436)
Scarce seven days I lived before the great
Dog-ape, the monkeys' chief, castrated me.
Such was the fruit of my lasciviousness. (437)
Therefrom deceasing in the woods of Sindh,
Reborn the offspring of a one-eyed goat (438)
And lame; twelve years a gelding, gnawn by worms,
Unfit, I carried children on my back.
Such was the fruit of my lasciviousness. (439)
Therefrom deceasing, I again found birth,
The offspring of a cattle-dealer's cow,
A calf of lac-red hue; in the twelfth month (440)
Castrated, yoked, I drew the plough and cart,
Purblind and worried, driven and unfit.
Such was the fruit of my lasciviousness. (441)
Therefrom deceasing, even in the street
I came to birth, child of a household slave,
Neither of woman nor of man my sex.
Such was the fruit of my lasciviousness. (442)
At thirty years of age I died, and was reborn
A girl, the daughter of a carter, poor
And of ill-fortune, and oppressed with debts
Incurred to usurers. To pay the sum (443)
Of interest that ever grew and swelled,
In place of money, [408]woeful little me

The merchant of a caravan dragged off,
Bearing me weeping from my home. (444)
Now in my sixteenth year, when I
Blossomed a maiden, that same merchant's son,
Giridāsa the name of him, loved me
And made me wife. Another wife he had, (445)
A virtuous dame of parts and of repute,
Enamoured of her mate. And thus I brought
Discord and enmity within that house. (446)

Fruit of my karma was it thus that they,
In this last life, have slighted me, e'en tho'
I waited on them as their humble slave.

Well! of all that now have I made an end! (447)

PSALM OF THE GREAT CHAPTER

LXXIII
Sumedhā

SHE too, having made her resolve under former Buddhas, and heaping up good of age-enduring efficacy in this and that rebirth, thoroughly preparing the conditions of emancipation, was born, when Koṇāgamana was Buddha, in a clansman's family. When she was of age, she and her friends, clansmen's daughters, agreed together to have a great park made, and handed it over to the Buddha and his Order. Through the merit of that act, she was reborn in the heaven of the Three-and-Thirty. After a glorious period there, she arose once more among the Yāma gods, then among the Blissful gods, then among the Happy Creators, then among the Disposers of others' creations, [409]and there became Queen of the King of the gods. Reborn thereafter, when Kassapa was Buddha, as the daughter of a wealthy citizen, she acquired splendid merit as a lay-believer, winning another rebirth among the gods of the Three-and-Thirty. Finally reborn, in this Buddha-age, at the city of Mantāvatī, as the daughter of King Koñca, [410]she was named Sumedhā. And when she was come to years of discretion, her mother and father agreed to let Anikaratta, the Rāja of Vāraṇavatī, see her. But she from her childhood had been in the habit of going with Princesses of her own age and attendant slaves to the Bhikkhunīs' quarters to hear them preach the Doctrine, and for a long time, because of her pristine resolve, she had grown fearful of birth in the round of life, devoted to religion and averse to the pleasures of sense.

Wherefore, when she heard the decision of her parents and kinsfolk, she said: 'My duty lies not in the life of the house. I will leave the world.' And they were not able to dissuade her. She thinking, 'Thus shall I gain permission to leave the world,' laid hold of her purpose, and cut off her own hair. Then using her hair in accordance with what she had heard from the Bhikkhunīs of their methods, she concentrated her attention on repugnance to physical attraction, and calling up the idea of 'Foul Things,' [411] then and there attained First Jhāna. And when she was thus rapt, her parents came to her apartments in order to give her away. But she made them first and all their retinue and all the Raja's people believers in religion, and left the house, renouncing the world in the Bhikkhunīs' quarters.

Not long after, establishing insight, and ripe for emancipation, she attained Arahantship, with thorough grasp of the Norm in form and in meaning. And reflecting on her victory, she broke forth in exultation:

> King Heron's daughter at Mantāvatī,
> Born of his chief consort, was Sumedhā,
> Devoted to the makers of the Law. [412](448)
> A virtuous maid was she and eloquent,
> Learnèd and in the system of our Lord
> Well trained. She of her parents audience sought,
> And spake: 'Now listen, mother, father, both! (449)
> All my heart's love is to Nibbana given.
> Transient is everything that doth become,
> E'en if it have the nature of a god.
> What truck have I, then, with the empty life
> Of sense, that giveth little, slayeth much? (450)
> Bitter as serpents' poison are desires
> Of sense, whereafter youthful fools do yearn.
> For that full many a night in wretchedness

They drag out tortured lives in realms of woe. [413](451)
The vicious-minded, vicious doers mourn
In purgatorial lives. Ever are fools
Without restraint in deed and word and thought. (452)
Oh! but the foolish have no wit or will.
They cannot grasp what maketh sorrow rise–
When taught, they learn not; in their slumb'ring minds
The Fourfold Ariyan Truth awakens not. (453)
Those Truths, O mother, that th' Awakened One,
The Best, the Buddha, hath revealed to us,
They, the Majority, know not, and they
Delight in coming aye again to be,
And long to be reborn among the gods. (454)
E'en with the gods is no eternal home. [414]
Becoming needs must be impermanent.
Yet they, the foolish souls, are not afraid
Again, again to come somewhere to birth. (455)
Four are the ways of doleful life, and two
Alone the ways of weal [415] –and these how hard
To win! Nor if one come into the four,
Is there renunciation from that world. (456)
Suffer ye both that I renounce my world;
And in the blessed teaching of the Lord,
Him of the Powers Ten, [416]heedless of all
Without, I'll strive to root out birth and death. (457)
How can I take delight in many births,
In this poor body, froth without a soul? [417]
That I may put an utter end to thirst
Again to be, suffer that I go forth. (458)
Now is the Age of Buddhas! Gone the want
Of opportunity! The moment's won!
O let me never while I live misprize
The precepts, nor withstand the holy life!' (459)

Thus spake Sumedhā, and again: 'Mother

And father mine, never again will I
As a laywoman break my fast and eat.
Here will I sooner lay me down and die!' (460)

Th' afflicted mother wept; the father, stunned
With grief, strove to dissuade and comfort her
Who prostrate lay upon the palace floor:– (461)
'Rise up, dear child. Why this unhappiness
For thee? Thou art betrothed to go and reign
In Vāraṇavatī, the promised bride
Of King Anikaratta, handsome youth. (462)
Thou art to be his chief consort, his queen.
Hard is it, little child, to leave the world,
Hard are the precepts and the holy life. (463)
As queen thou wilt enjoy authority,
Riches and sov'reignty and luxuries.
Thou that art blest herein and young, enjoy
The sweets life yields. Let's to thy wedding, child.' (464)

Then answered them Sumedhā: 'Nay, not thus!
No soul, no essence, can becoming yield.
One or the other shall be–choose ye which:
Or let me leave the world, or let me die.
Thus, and thus only, would I choose to wed. [418](465)
What is it worth [419] –this body foul, unclean,
Emitting odours, source of fears, a bag
Of skin with carrion filled, oozing impure (466)
The while? What is it worth to me who know–
Repulsive carcass, plastered o'er with flesh
And blood, the haunt of worms, dinner of birds–
To whom shall such a thing as this be given? (467)
Borne in a little while to charnel-field,
There is this body thrown, when mind hath sped, [420]
Like useless log, from which e'en kinsfolk turn. (468)

Throwing the thing that they have bathed to be
The food of alien things, whereat recoil
The very parents, let alone their kin. (469)
They have a fondness for this soulless frame,
That's knit of bones and sinews, body foul,
Filled full of exudations manifold. (470)
Where one the body to dissect, and turn
The inside outermost, the smell would prove
Too much for e'en one's mother to endure. (471)
The factors of my being, organs, elements,
All are a transient compound, rooted deep
In birth, are Ill, and first and last the thing
I would not. [421]Whom, then, could I choose to wed?
(472)
Rather would I find death day after day
With spears three hundred piercing me anew,
E'en for an hundred years, if this would then
Put a last end to pain, unending else. (473)
The wise would with this [bargain] close, and meet
Utter destruction, seeing that His Word,
The Master's, runneth: "Long the wandering
Of them who, smitten, ever rise again." [422](474)
Countless the ways in which we meet our death,
'Mong gods and men, as demons or as beasts,
Among the shades, or in the haunts of hell.[423] (475)
And there how many doomed tormented live!
No sure refuge is ours even in heaven.
Above, beyond Nibbana's bliss, is naught. (476)
And they have won that Bliss who all their hearts
Have plighted to the blessed Word of Him
Who hath the Tenfold Power, and heeding naught,
Have striv'n to put far from them birth and death. (477)
This day, my father, will I get me forth!
I'll naught of empty riches! Sense-desires
Repel and sicken me, and are become

E'en as the stump where once hath stood a palm.' (478)

So spake she to her father. Now the King,
Anikaratta, on his way to woo
His youthful bride's consent, drew near
At the appointed time. But Sumedhā (479)
Let down the soft black masses of her hair
And with a dagger cut them off. Then closed
The door that led to her own terraced rooms,
And forthwith to First Jhana-rapture won. (480)
There sat she lost in ecstasy, the while
Anikaratta reached the capital.
Then she fell musing on impermanence,
Developing the thought. [424]Then is she ware (481)
The while Anikaratta swiftly mounts
The palace steps, in brave array of gems
And gold, and bowing low woos Sumedhā. (482)

'Reign in my kingdom and enjoy my wealth
And power. Rich, happy and so young thou art,
Enjoy the sweets that life and love can yield,
Though they be hard to win and won by few. (483)
To thee my kingdom I surrender! Now
Dispose as thou dost wish, give gifts galore.
Be not downcast. Thy parents are distressed.' (484)

To him thus Sumedhā, for whom desires
Of sensuous love were worthless, nor availed
To lead astray, made answer: 'O set not
The heart's affections on this sensual love.
See all the peril, the satiety of sense. (485)
Mandhātā, King o' th' world's four continents, [425]
Had greater wealth to gratify his sense
Than any other man, yet passed away

Unsatisfied, his wishes unfulfilled. (486)
Nay, an the rain-god rained all seven kinds
Of gems till earth and heaven were full, still would
The senses crave, and men insatiate die. (487)
'Like the sharp blades of swords are sense-desires.'
'Like the poised heads of snakes prepared to dart.'
'Like blazing torches,' and 'like bare gnawn bones.' [426]
(488)
Transient, unstable are desires of sense,
Pregnant with Ill and full of venom dire,
Searing as heated iron globe to touch.
Baneful the root of them, baleful the fruit. (489)
As 'fruit' [427] that brings the climber to a fall,
Are sense-desires; evil as 'lumps of flesh'
That greedy birds one from the other snatch;
As cheating 'dreams'; as 'borrowed goods' reclaimed.
(490)
'As spears and jav'lins are desires of sense,'
'A pestilence, a boil, and bane and bale.
A furnace of live coals,' the root of bane,
Murderous and the source of harrowing dread. (491)

So hath the direfulness of sense-desires,
Those barriers to salvation, been declared.
Go, leave me, for I do not trust myself,
While in this world I yet have part and lot. (492)
What shall another do for me? For me
Whose head is wrapped in flames, [428]whose steps are
dogged
By age and death that tarry not. To crush
Them utterly I needs must strive.' (493)

Then coming to her door she saw the king
Her suitor, and her parents seated there

And shedding tears. And once more spake to them:
(494)

'Long have they yet to wander through the worlds
Who witless aye again their tears renew,
Weeping world without end for father dead,
Or brother slain, or that themselves must die. [429](495)
Call ye to mind how it was said that tears
And milk and blood flow on world without end.
And bear in mind that tumulus of bones
By creatures piled who wander through the worlds.
(496)
Remember the four oceans as compared
With all the flow of tears and milk and blood.
Remember the 'great cairn of one man's bones
From one æon alone, equal to Vipula'; (497)
And how 'great India [430] would not suffice
To furnish little tally-balls of mould,
Wherewith to number all the ancestors
Of one's own round of life world without end.' (498)
Remember how 'the little squares of straws
And boughs and twigs could ne'er suffice
As tallies for one's sires world without end.' (499)
Remember how the parable was told
Of 'purblind turtle in the Eastern Seas,
Or other oceans, once as time goes by,
Thrusting his head thro' hole of drifting yoke';
So rare as this the chance of human birth. [431](500)
Remember too the 'body'-parable,
The 'lump of froth,' of spittle without core,
Drifting. See here the fleeting factors five.
And O forget not hell where many thole. (501)
Remember how we swell the charnel-fields,
Now dying, now again elsewhere reborn.

Remember what was said of 'crocodiles,' [432]
And what those perils meant for us, and O!
Bear ye in mind the Four, the Ariyan Truths. (502)

THE NECTAR OF THE NORM IS HERE! [433]O how
Canst thou be satisfied with bitter draughts
Of sense satiety? All sensual joys
Are bitterer for the fivefold dogging Ill. [434](503)

THE NECTAR OF THE NORM IS HERE! O how
Canst thou be satisfied with fevered fits
Of sense-satiety? All sensual joys
Are burning, boiling, ferment, [435]stew. (504)

THERE IS, WHERE ENMITY IS NOT! [436]O how
Canst thou be satisfied with joys of sense
Engend'ring thee so many foes–the wrath
Or greed of king, or thief, or rival, harm
Through fire, or water–yea, so many foes! (505)

EMANCIPATION [437] WAITS! O how canst thou
Be satisfied with sensual joys, wherein
Lie bonds and death? Yea, in those very joys
Lurk gaol and headsman. [438]They who seek t' indulge
Their lusts needs must thereafter suffer ills. (506)
Him will straw-torches burn who holds them long
And lets not go. So, in the parable, [439]
Desires of sense burn them who let not go. (507)
Cast not away, because of some vain joy
Of sense, the vaster happiness sublime,
Lest like the finny carp thou gulp the hook,
Only to find thyself for that foredone [440] (508)
Tame thou thyself in sense-desires, nor let
Thyself be bound by them, as is a dog
Bound by a chain; else will they do forsooth

With thee as hungry pariahs with that dog. [441](509)
Once more I say, immeasurable Ills
And many weary miseries of mind
Thou'lt suffer yoked to sensual life. Renounce,
Renounce desires of sense! They pass away. (510)

THERE IS, THAT GROWETH NEVER OLD! [442]O how
Canst thou be satisfied with sense-desires
That age so soon? Are not all things reborn,
Where'er it be, gripped by disease and death? (511)
THIS [443] that doth ne'er grow old, that dieth not,
THIS never-ageing, never-dying Path–
No sorrow cometh there, no enemies,
Nor is there any crowd; [444]none faint or fail,
No fear cometh, nor aught that doth torment– (512)
To THIS, the Path Ambrosial, have gone
Full many. And to-day, e'en now 'tis to be won.
But only by a life that's utterly
Surrendered in devotion. Labour not,
And ye shall not attain!'

Thus Sumedhā (513)
Ended her say, who found no joy in all
Activities that lead from life to life,
And, to Anikaratta thus her mind
Declaring, dropped her tresses on the floor. (514)
Then up he rose with outstretched folded hands,
And with her father pleaded for her thus:
'O suffer Sumedhā to leave the world,
That she may see the Truth and Liberty!' (515)

The parents suffered her, and forth she went,
Afeared to stay and build up fear and grief.
Six branches of Insight she realized,

As learner, winning to the Topmost Fruit. (516)

O wondrous this! O marvellous in sooth!
Nibbāna for the daughter of a king!
Her state and conduct in her former births,
E'en as she told in her last life were these: (517)
'When [445] Koṇāgamana was Buddha here,
And in a new abode, the Order's Park,
Took up his dwelling, two o' my friends, [446]and I
Built a Vihāra for the Master's use. (518)
And many scores and centuries of lives
We lived among the gods, let alone men. (519)
Mighty our glory and our power among
The gods, nor need I speak of fame on earth.
Was I not consort of an Emperor,
The Treasure-Woman 'mongst the Treasures Seven? [447](520)

Endurance [448] in the Truth the Master taught–
This was the cause, the source, the root,
This the First Link in the long Causal Line,
This is Nibbana if we love the Norm. (521)

Thus acting, [449]they who put their trust in Him,
Wisdom Supreme, [450]lose every wish and hope
Of coming back to be–and thus released
They from all passion's stain are purified. [451](522)

COMMENTATOR'S ENVOI

The Psalms of them who through the Gospel's grace
Became the true-born children and the heirs,
Mouth-born, of Him who is the Master Blest,
King o' the Norm, creations of the Norm,
Excelling in all virtue, Arahants,

Who wrought all that 'twas possible to do–
These Psalms, their utterances when AÑÑĀ
They did proclaim, or whensoe'er it was,
Beginning with Brother SUBHŪTI'S verse,
With Sisters Psalms, headed by 'STURDYKIN'–
All these the Leaders of the Order took,
And in one ordered serial compiled,
The THERAGĀTHĀ-THERĪGĀTHĀ named.

To elucidate the import of that work
Three Older Commentaries are extant. [452]
Thereto this exegesis I have tried
T' indite, the which, in that where'er 'twas fit,
I strove to set the highest meaning forth,
I named the Paramattha-Dīpanī;
The whole whereof, now finished to the end,
By orderly decision is arranged,
For recitation from the sacred text,
In chapters of the number ninety-two.
Thus by the efficacy of such good
As has accrued to me, by me applied,
Have I made bright the glory of the word,
The system, of the Sovran of the world;
That, by their pure attainment in all truth
And virtue, mortals all may come to taste
The essence of emancipation won.
Long may the Very Buddha's Word and Law
Abide, and ever may it be revered
By every creature that hath life and breath!
And may the weather-god in season due
Send rain on earth, and may the powers that be
Govern the world as lovers of the Norm!

Thus endeth the Commentary on the Therigāthā, by the Teacher, Brother Dhammapāla, residing at the Padara-Tittha-Vihāra.

APPENDIX

1. Āḷavikā. [453]

THUS have I heard. The Exalted One was once staying at Sāvatthī, in the Jeta Grove, the park of Anāthapiṇḍika. Now Āḷavikā the Bhikkhunī dressed herself early and, taking bowl and robe, entered Sāvatthī for food. And when she had gone about Sāvatthī for it, had broken her fast and returned, she entered the Dark Wood, seeking solitude.

Then Māra the Evil One, desiring to arouse fear, wavering, and dread in her, desiring to make her desist from being alone, went up to her, and addressed her in a verse:

'Ne'er shalt thou find escape while in the world.
What profiteth thee then thy loneliness?
Take the good things of life while yet thou may'st,
Repentance else too late awaiteth thee.'

Then Āḷavikā thought: 'Who now is this, human or non-human, that speaketh this verse? Sure 'tis Māra the Evil One speaketh it, desirous to arouse in me fear, wavering and dread, desirous to make me desist from my solitude.' And Bhikkhunī Āḷavikā, knowing that 'twas he, replied with a verse:

'There is escape while in the world, and I
Have well attained thereto by insight won.
Thou evil limb of loafing! [454]'tis not thine
To know that bourne, or how it may be reached.
Like spears and jav'lins are the joys of sense,

That pierce and rend the mortal frames of us.
These that thou callest "the good things of life,"
Good of that ilk to me is nothing worth.'

Then Māra, thinking, 'Bhikkhunī Āḷavikā knows me!' vanished thence, sad and dejected.

2. Somā. [455]

. . . . . [456]Now Somā . . . . . entered the Dark Wood for siesta, and, plunging into its depths, sat down at the root of a certain tree for siesta.

Then Māra the Evil One, desiring to arouse fear, wavering, and dread in her, desiring to make her desist from concentrated thought, went up to her, and addressed her in a verse:

'That vantage-ground the sages may attain is hard
To reach. With her two-finger consciousness
That is no woman competent to gain!'

Then Somā thought . . . . . 'Sure 'tis Māra!'. . . . and replied with verses:

'What should the woman's nature do to them [457]
Whose hearts are firmly set, who ever move
With growing knowledge onward in the Path?
What can that signify to one in whom
Insight doth truly comprehend the Norm?
To one for whom the question doth arise:
Am I a woman in these matters, or
Am I a man, or what not am I, then?
To such an one is Māra fit to talk!'

Then Māra, thinking, 'Bhikkhunī Somā knows me,' vanished thence, sad and dejected.

3. Gotamī. [458]

. . . . . Now the Lean Gotamid . . . . . entered the Dark Wood for siesta, and, plunging into its depths, sat down at the root of a certain tree for siesta. Then Māra . . . . . went up to her, and addressed her in a verse:

'How now? Dost sit alone with tearful face
As mother stricken by the loss of child?
Thou who hast plunged into the woods alone,
Is it a man that thou hast come to seek?'

Then the Lean Gotamid thought . . . . . 'Sure 'tis Māra!' . . . . . and replied with verses:

'Ay, ever am I she whose child is lost! [459]
And for the seeking, there are men at hand.
I do not grieve, I am not shedding tears,
And as for thee, good sir, I fear thee not.
Slain everywhere is love of worldly joys,
And the thick gloom of ignorance is rent in twain.
Defeating all the army of the power of death,
I here abide purged of the poison-drugs.' [460]

Then Māra, thinking, 'Bhikkhunī Gotamī knows me!' vanished thence, sad and dejected.

4. Vijayā. [461]

. . . . . Now Bhikkhunī Vijayā . . . . . sat down at the root of a certain tree for siesta.

Then Māra . . . . . addressed her in a verse: [462]

'A maiden thou and beautiful–and I
So young a lad! Now where to fivefold art [463]
Of sounds melodious we may list, O come,
Lady, and let us take our fill of joy!'

Then Bhikkhunī Vijayā thought . . . . . 'Sure 'tis Māra!' . . . . . and . . . . . replied with verses:

'Sights, sounds and tastes and smells and things to touch,
Wherein the mind delights, I leave them all
To thee, Māra; for such no mind have I!
This body vile, this brittle, crumbling thing,
Doth touch me only with distress and shame.
Craving for joys of sense is rooted out.
They who have come to worlds of form, and they
Who dwell where form is not, and that perfect
Attainment which is peace [464] –from all,
From everywhere, the darkness is dispelled.'

Then Māra, thinking, 'Bhikkhunī Vijayā knows me!' vanished thence, sad and dejected.

5. Uppalavaṇṇā.

. . . . . Now, Bhikkhunī Uppalavaṇṇā . . . . . entered the Dark Wood for siesta, and, plunging into its depths, halted at the root of a certain sāla-tree in full blossom.

Then Māra . . . . . addressed her in a verse:

'Thou that art come where over thee crownèd with blossom
[Waveth] the sāl-tree, Sister, and standest alone in the shade of it,
No one like thee could hither come rival to beauty as thine is!
Fearest thou not, O foolish maiden, the wiles of seducers?' [465]

Then Bhikkhunī Uppalavaṇṇā thought . . . . . 'Sure 'tis Māra!' . . . . . and . . . . . replied with verses:

'Were there an hundred thousand seducers e'en such as thou art,
Ne'er would I tremble affrighted thereat, or turn a hair of me.
Māra, I fear not thee, all lonely though I be standing.
Here though I stand, I vanish, or enter into thy body.
See! 'twixt thine eyelashes hide, standing where thou canst not see me.
For all my mind is wholly self-controlled,
And the Four Paths to Potency are thoroughly learnt.
Yea, I am free from all the Bonds there be.
In sooth, good sir, no fear have I of thee!'

Then Māra, thinking, 'Bhikkhunī Uppalavaṇṇā knows me!' vanished thence, sad and dejected.

6. Cālā. [466]

. . . . . Now, Bhikkhunī Cālā . . . . . sat down at the root of a certain tree for siesta.

Then Māra the Evil One went up to her, and spoke thus to her: 'Wherein, O Sister, dost thou find no pleasure?'

'In birth, [467]good sir, I find no pleasure.'

'Why findest thou no pleasure in birth? Once born, one enjoys the pleasures of a life of sense. Who hath put this into thy mind–"Find no pleasure in birth"–Sister?'

> 'Once born, we die. Once born, we see life's Ills–
> The bonds, the torments, and the life cut off. [468]
> The Buddha hath revealed the Norm to us–
> How we may get beyond the power of birth,
> How we may put an end to every Ill.
> 'Tis He hath guided me into the True.
> They who have come to worlds of Form, and they
> Who in those worlds abide where Form is not,
> An they know not how they may end it all,
> Are goers, all of them, again to birth. [469]

Then Māra, thinking, 'Bhikkhunī Cālā knows me!' vanished thence, sad and dejected.

7. Upacālā. [470]

. . . . . Now, Bhikkhunī Upacālā . . . . . sat down at the root of a certain tree for siesta.

Then Māra the Evil One, desiring to arouse fear . . . . . to make her desist from concentrated thought, went up to her, and spoke thus to her:

> 'Where, Sister, dost thou wish to rise again?'
>
> 'Nowhere, good sir, I wish to rise again.'

'Now, think upon the Three-and-Thirty gods,
And on the gods who rule in realm of Shades,
On those who reign in Heaven of Bliss, and on
Those higher deities who live where life
Yet flows by way of sense and of desire–
Think, and thither aspire with longing heart,
The bliss of each in turn shall then be thine.'

Upacālā.

Ay, think upon the Three-and-Thirty gods,
And on the gods who rule in realm of Shades,
On those who reign in Heaven of Bliss, and on
Those higher deities who live where life
Yet flows by way of sense and of desire!
They all are bound by bonds of sense-desire,
Hence come they evermore 'neath Māra's sway.
On fire is all the world, is wrapt in smoke. [471]
Ablaze is all the world, the heav'ns do quake!
But that which quaketh not, influctuate, [472]
Untrodden by the average worldling's feet,
Where Māra cometh not nor hath way-gate–
There doth my heart abide in blest retreat.' [473]

Then Māra, thinking, 'Bhikkhunī Upacālā knows me!' vanished thence, sad and dejected.

8. Sīsupacālā. [474]

. . . . . Now, Bhikkhunī Sīsupacālā . . . . . sat down at the root of a certain tree for siesta.

Then Māra the Evil One went up to her, and spoke to her thus: 'Of whose shibboleth, Sister, dost thou approve?' 'I approve of no one's shibboleth, good sir.'

'Why now and whereto art thou seen thus garbed
And shaven like a nun, yet dost not join
Ascetics of some sort and shibboleth?
What, futile and infatuate, is thy quest?'

''Tis they that are without, caught in the net
Of the vain shibboleths in which they trust–
Their's is the doctrine I cannot approve.
'Tis they that lack acquaintance with the Norm.

'Lo! in the princely Sākiya clan is born
A Buddha peerless 'mong the sons of men,
Who all hath overcome, before whose face
Māra doth flee away, who everywhere
Unconquered stands, He that is wholly freed
And fetterless, the Seer who seeth all,
For whom all karma is destroyed, who in
The perishing of every germ that birth
Once more engenders, is at liberty.
This the Exalted One, my Master and my Lord:
His doctrine, His the word that I approve.'

Then Māra, thinking, 'Bhikkhunī Sīsupacālā knows me! . . . . .

9. Selā. [475]

. . . . . Now, Bhikkhunī Selā . . . . . sat down at the root of a certain tree for siesta.

Then Māra . . . . . went up to her, and addressed her with a verse:

'Who was't that made this human puppet's form?
Where, tell me, is the human doll's artificer?
Whence hath the human puppet come to be?
Where, tell me, shall it cease and pass away?'

Then Bhikkhunī Selā thought . . . . . ' Sure 'tis Māra!' . . . . . and . . . . . replied with verses:

'Neither self-made the puppet is, nor yet
By other is this evil fashionèd.
By reason of a cause it came to be;
By rupture of a cause, it dies away.
Like to a given seed sown in the field,
Which, when it lighteth on the taste of earth
And moisture likewise–by these twain doth grow,
So the five aggregates, the elements,
And the six spheres of sense–even all these–
By reason of a cause they came to be;
By rupture of a cause they die away.'

Then Māra, thinking, 'Bhikkhunī Selā knows me!' vanished thence, sad and dejected.

10. Vajirā.

. . . . . Now Bhikkhunī Vajirā . . . . . sat down at the root of a certain tree for siesta.

Then Māra . . . . . went up to her, and addressed her with a verse:

'Who hath this being [476] fashioned? Where is
The maker of this being? Whence hath it sprung?

Where doth this being cease and pass away?'

Then Bhikkhunī Vajirā thought . . . . . 'Sure 'tis Māra!' . . . . . and replied with a verse:

'"Being"? Why dost thou harp upon that word?
'Mong false opinions, Māra, art thou strayed.
This a mere bundle of formations is.
Therefrom no "being" mayest thou obtain.
For e'en as, when the factors are arranged,
The product by the word "chariot" is known,
So doth our usage covenant to say–
"A being"–when the aggregates are there.
''Tis simply Ill that riseth, simply Ill
That doth persist, and then fadeth away.
Nought beside Ill it is that doth become;
Nought else but Ill it is doth pass away.'

Then Māra, thinking, 'Bhikkhunī Vajirā knows me!' vanished thence, sad and dejected.

The Yakkha-Saŋyutta, or Fairy Series in the same Nikāya, gives the summons uttered by the indignant tree-fairy to the people of Rājagaha in Sukkā's little poem (Ps. xxxiv.). The lines are exactly the same, except that 'wayfarer' is panthagū instead of addhagū.

In the following Sutta presumably the same devoted spirit proclaims the praises both of Sukkā and of a lay-disciple who supplied the eloquent Therī with food:

'O surely plenteous merit hath he wrought,
That layman wise, who Sukkā's wants supplied–
Sukkā's, who from all bonds is wholly free!' [477]

NOTES

I. On clansmen, to which reference is so often made in the Chronicles (clansman's family=kulageha), see Rhys Davids, Buddhist India, 17-22. 'Treasurer' or 'merchant' stands for seṭṭhi, a leading commoner, head (seṭṭhi=chief) of a guild, and often treasurer to a King.

II. On the co-existing customs of cremation and exposure of the dead, to which the Psalms testify, see Rhys Davids, Buddhist India, 78 f.

III. In the note on p. 66, reference should have been made to the Viticcha-jātaka, No. 244, in the second volume of the Jātaka. Here the Buddha himself asks the question, Ekaŋ nāma kiŋ? whereupon the itinerant debater runs away! The birth-story is then told, the question being contra the theory of the Ding-an-sich.

CORRIGENDUM

In verse 72, where Professors Pischel and E. Müller have read

... aññā samatimaññi 'haŋ,
I now incline, with the Commentary, to read
aññāsam atimaññi 'haŋ,
and would amend the English thus:
Filled with the pride of my youth, I scorned and despised other women.

Again, in verse 74, a truer rendering would be:

Manifold wiles I wrought, mocking with insolent laughter.

And in verse 76, for 'calm' read 'cool.'

ENDNOTES

---

[1] The Thera- and Therī-Gāthā: Stanzas ascribed to Elders of the Buddhist Order of Recluses. London, 1883. (p. 2)

[2] Paramattha-Dīpanī, Part V. London, 1893. Discussed by me at the Ninth Congress of Orientalists, London, 1892 (Transactions, i., p. 393. London, 1893). (p. 2)

[3] This work consists of commentaries on the canonical works, entitled Udāna, Vimāna-vatthu, Peta-vatthu, beside the two under discussion. (p. 2)

[4] Die Lieder der Mönche und Nonnen Gotamo Buddho's. Berlin, 1899. (p. 3)

[5] The Jātaka, or Stories of the Buddha's Former Births. 6 vols. Cambridge, 1895-1907. (p. 4)

[6] Johnson defines 'psalm' as 'a holy song.' There is no indication of 'psaltery' having accompanied the recitation of canonical gāthās. (p. 4)

[7] He rewrote in Pali what had been handed down in Sinhalese, or perhaps in Tamil. (p. 4)

[8] See below, p. 178: porāṇaṭṭhakathā-tayaŋ. (p. 4)

[9] I have judged it best not to overload this volume by translating the Apadāna verses. They are adduced to confirm the attha-kathā with the words, 'As it is said in the Apadāna.' This work is now being edited by Mrs. Mabel Bode, Ph.D., for the Pali Text Society. (p. 4)

---

[10] Omitting the two poems ascribed to the followers of Paṭācārā collectively, and assuming that certain poems attributed to Sisters with the same name are by different persons. (p. 5)

[11] Professor Windisch concludes that these ten Psalms were taken from an old collection of Māra legends (Māra und Buddha, 134). (p. 5)

[12] Translated in Rhys Davids's Buddhist Birth Stories. See especially pp. 12-14. (p. 7)

[13] Windisch, Māra und Buddha, pp. 222 ff.; Rhys Davids, Buddhist India, pp. 177-186. (p. 7)

[14] Cf. verses 16, 18; 14, 20; 38, 41; 59, 62, 188, 195, 203, 235; latter part of 112, 117, 175; 120, 173, 179, 180, etc. (p. 8)

[15] See Professor E. Müller's Introduction, Paramatthadīpanī, xiv., xv. (p. 8)

[16] In one of the shorter Psalms (xlviii.) the narrative form emerges: 'The Thirty Sisters heard, and swift obeyed,' etc. (p. 9)

[17] Therīgāthā, Preface. (p. 9)

[18] Zeitschrift der D. M. G., 37, 54 ff., especially pp. 77-82. (p. 9)

[19] See verse 431 n. (p. 10)

[20] One brief poem makes a bare allusion of this nature, verse 40 n. (p. 10)

[21] The Kathā Vatthu, in the Abhidhamma-Pitaka, compiled by Moggaliputta Tissa in the reign of the Emperor Asoka. (p. 10)

[22] Rhys Davids, Buddhist India, p. 179. (p. 10)

[23] Op. cit., Introduction. (p. 10)

[24] We may ignore for present purposes the pious humility which ascribed several shorter gāthās to the Buddha himself. (p. 10)

[25] 'The bidding of the Buddha is done'; 'the Threefold Lore is won'; 'rebirth comes now no more.' (p. 11)

[26] The Inner Shrine. (p. 12)

[27] Ps. lxx., verse 349; cf. Ps, xi., xl. (p. 12)

[28] Ps. xi., xxi. (p. 13)

[29] Ps. xxiv. (p. 13)

[30] Ps. xvi. (p. 14)

[31] Ps. xviii. (p. 15)

[32] Sāmī, sāmiko, pati mean equally owner, lord, husband. (p. 15)

[33] Ps. lxiii. I.e., physically frail or lean. (p. 16)

[34] Pronounoe c like ch in 'church.' (p. 16)

[35] In Memoriam, vi. (p. 16)

[36] Cf. Ps. xxxiii., Ubbirī. (p. 17)

[37] The fact that bhavanga in this sense occurs frequently in the Commentaries, and, earlier still, in Milinda, and in Netti-Pakaraṇa (where a bodily and a mental continuum are distinguished, 91), but not in the Pitakas, is not wholly without chronological significance. (p. 18)

[38] L. Eckenstein, Women under Monasticism, p. 486. (p. 19)

---

[39] Ps. li., v. 138 (p. 19)

[40] On the term Amata, Cf. Questions of Milinda (S.B.E.), Vol. i. 236. The word 'state' in connection with it does not occur in the Psalms. (p. 19)

[41] Eckenstein, op. cit., pp. 253, 307 ff, 486. (p. 20)

[42] 'Tuvaŋ Buddho tuvaŋ Satthā, tuyhaŋ dhīt amhi brahmaṇa Orasā mukhato jātā. . . .' (Ps. lxix., verse 336). (p. 20)

[43] Ps. xxxi.; Ps. lxxi., verse 384. (p. 21)

[44] Anguttara Nikāya, i. 25. (p. 21)

[45] 'The loose woman and the nun . . . have this in common, that they are both the outcome of the refusal among womankind to accept married relations on the basis of the subjection imposed by the fatherage' (L. Eckenstein, op. cit., 5). (p. 21)

[46] Ps. xlviii.-l., 1viii., xxx. xxxiv., xxxviii., lxx. (p. 21)

[47] William Watson. As I have said elsewhere, Matthew Arnold's lines in Rugby Chapel might have been written of the Therī's:

'Ye like angels appear,
Radiant with ardour divine;
Beacons of hope ye appear;
Languor is not in your heart,
Weakness is not in your word,
Weariness not on your brow.' (p. 22)

[48] V. Hugo, L'Âne. (p. 22)

[49] Ps. lxxii.: '. . . tassa pi anto kato mayā!' Isidāsī.
'Even of that now have I made an end.' (p. 23)

[50] W. Watson, Wordsworth's Grave. The English poet and the Buddhist spirit here embrace. Santi or Samatha (peace, calm) is closely allied by the latter with Vipassanā (clear sight, insight); and with all good thought is involved also Samādhi or Jhāna (contemplative rapture), and often Pīti (emotional rapture), the Indriya's (or Bala's, powers) and Adosa (or Mettā, love). (p. 23)

[51] This word is in some respects a more adequate translation of Dhamma (Sanskrit, Dharma) than Law, Truth, or Gospel. By Dhamma is meant one of the five cosmic orders or sequences of happenings in the universe. Beside the order of action (kamma), of the physical forces (utu), of biological forces (bīja, or germs), and of mind, there was, if one may so call it, the moral or regenerative cosmos–dhamma-niyama–by which the living universe evolved its Buddhas and toiled upward out of the eternal round of saŋsāra towards salvation and the ideal. These five are severally declared in the Canon, but were classified later. See Buddhaghosa's Commentary on Dīgha Nikāya, Sutta xiv. (p. 23)

[52] Ps. lxv., li., xxxiv., xii. (p. 23)

[53] Ps. xlvi., xlii. (p. 24)

[54] This twofold classification must, of course, not be taken absolutely. It is merely a question of relative emphasis–e.g., B 1 (a) is equally a getting rid of the 'Darkness' of Ignorance. (p. 25)

[55] Sumedhā was evidently a born preacher! (p. 26)

[56] I refer readers to the deeply interesting opening chapter in Miss Eckenstein's book, Women under Monasticism. (p. 26)

[57] Dr. Jane Harrison, Prolegomena to Greek Religion, pp. 239 ff. (p. 27)

[58] Saccavādivacanaŋ anaññthā. (p. 27)

[59] E.g., in Ps. lxiii. (see p. 110, n. 2); Ps. xxi.:

Sumuttike sumuttikā sādhu muttikāmhi musalassa;'

and the last poem, beginning:

'Mantāvatiyā nagare raññо Koñcassa aggamahesiyā.'

Cf. in verse 512 the curious rhythm:

'I d a m a j a r aŋ i d a m a m a r aŋ i d a m a j a r ā m a r a p a d a m a s o k aŋ.' (p. 29)

60 One instance of unnecessarily 'free,' not to say incorrect, rendering, discovered too late for revision, I have amended on p. 192, slightly revising the Pali text. (p. 29)

61 Sutta Nipāta, verse 336. (p. 30)

62 One of the twenty-four Buddhas of later Buddhism. Early Buddhism reckoned only seven. For this and the following episodes in greater detail, cf. Rhys Davids, Buddhist Birth Stories, pp. 12 f. 27, 28; 60, 61; 87; 92. (p. 32)

63 Loc. cit., 87. (p. 33)

64 Ibid., 92 ff. (p. 33)

65 Loc. cit., 96. (p. 34)

66 =King's-stead Tree. (p. 34)

67 See Translator's Preface. (p. 34)

68 See his story in Ps. lxviii. (p. 34)

[69] Translated by Rhys Davids in Buddhist Suttas, S.B.E. xi., pp. 146 ff. (p. 34)

[70] Lit., territory–i.e., the 'true faith.' Cf. Buddhist Birth Stories, p. 113. (p. 35)

[71] Cf. Buddhist Birth Stories, p. 123 f. (p. 35)

[72] The sister and co-wife of the Buddha's mother. See Ps. lv. (p. 35)

[73] His half-brother (son of Pajāpatī), and his own son. (p. 35)

[74] I.e., as King and layman, without renouncing the world. (p. 35)

[75] For the oldest acoount of this, see Rhys Davids and Oldenberg, Vinaya Texts, iii., 320 f. (p. 36)

[76] Majjhima Nikāya, iii., pp. 270 ff. (p. 36)

[77] Koṇāgamana and Kassapa successively preceded Gotama as Buddhas. (p. 37)

[78] See Ps. xii. (p. 38)

[79] Muttā=freed (woman). (p. 38)

[80] Cf. the 'Ford' Jātaka (Buddhist Birth Stories, 253):
'He has gained freedom–as the moon set free,
When an eclipse has passed, from Rāhu's jaws.' (p. 38)

[81] Cf. Dialogues of the Buddha, i. 82-84. (p. 38)

[82] Gandha-kūṭi, the traditional term for the Buddha's own room, especially that at the Jetavana Vihāra, Sāvatthi. (p. 39)

[83] Cf. Ps. lxv., note. (p. 39)

[84] Ca=Cha. The word is equivalent to 'moonlight.' Cf. Ps. xxix., xxxii. (p. 39)

[85] A free rendering of Pacceka-Buddha–one enlightened for himself alone, not a world-Saviour. (p. 39)

[86] Puṇṇā='full.' (p. 39)

[87] The words 'holy life,' 'of the path,' 'of ignorance,' are from the Commentary. (p. 39)

[88] Pronounce Anyā = literally, her having come to know. A subjective synonym of Arahantship. (p. 39)

[89] There is more in this little poem than is at first sight apparent. Tissā–i.e., (a girl) born under the lucky star or constellation of Tissa, a celestial archer (partly identical with Cancer)–suggests a word-play on tisso sikkhāyo, the three branches of religious training (morals, mind, 'insight'). Again, that a word-play on yoga is intended is intelligible even without the Commentary. 'Let the lucky yoga (conjuncture)–to wit, your rebirth as human, your possession of all your faculties (read indriya-avekallaŋ), the advent of a Buddha, your getting conviction–not slip; for by this yoking of opportunities you can free yourself from the Four Yokes–viz., sense, renewed existence, opinion, ignorance–which bind you to the Wheel of Life. (p. 40)

[90] The Four Āsavas, or Intoxicants (another metaphor for the Four Bonds, or Yokes). (p. 40)

[91] Yogakkhema, a term adapted from secular use, therein meaning well-being or security in possession. (p. 40)

[92] Her name means 'brave,' 'heroic.' (p. 41)

[93] Mittā='friend'; but see note 2 to Ps. xxv. (p. 41)

[94] 'In thought and deed,' 'worthy of thy love,' are from the Commentary. 'Peace' is another rendering of yogakkhema, so is 'security' (verse 9). (p. 41)

[95] Bhadrā=Felicia. (p. 41)

[96] The graceful progression–bhadraratā bhava, bhāvehi . . . cannot well be reproduced. It is merely suggested by 'devote. Develop.' (p. 41)

[97] Upăsămā=tranquil, calm. (p. 41)

[98] Cf. Ps. ii (p. 42)

[99] The Thera Sumangala also celebrates his release from three crooked things–the sickle, the plough, and the spade. See Ps. xxi. (p. 42)

[100] The seven most illustrious women of early Buddhism have been grouped as these Seven Sisters in the Apadāna: Khemā, Uppalavaṇṇā, Paṭācārā, Bhaddā (Ps. xlvi.), Kisāgotamī, Dhammadinnā, and Visākhā, the wealthy lay sister. On the last see Warren, Buddhism in Translations, 451 f. (p. 43)

[101] Literally, 'together with the Paṭisambhidā's,' or four aspects of doctrinal knowledge. These four–analytical knowledge in meaning, doctrine, interpretation, and distinctions–are very variously interpreted, both in works of Abhidhamma content (Paṭisambhidāmagga, Vibhanga) and in commentarial writings of various later dates (see Childers's Dictionary, s.v.). The phrase is of commentarial date, and recurs frequently in Dhammapāla (see following Psalms). (p. 44)

[102] In the Majjhima Nikāya, i., p. 299 ff.; discussed by the writer in J.R.A.S., 1894, p. 321. Cf. Mrs. Bode in J.R.A.S., 1893, p. 562 ff. (p. 44)

[103] In the mythology of Buddhism respecting the after-life, the Uddhaŋ-soto was one who, having destroyed here below only the first five of the ten Fetters (to destroy all ten meant Nibbana in this life), was reborn successively in an ever higher heaven, till, reaching the

Supreme or Akaniṭṭha Sphere, he there passed away. The expression means rather rising above the stream of saŋsāra than going against it; but it is ambiguous, and, anyway, the upward effort is expressed in either metaphor. The Commentary has, as the last word, not ti vuccati ('is called'), but vimuccati ('is set free'). As it does not comment on the latter term, I incline to hold it a misreading. (p. 44)

[104] Ps. vi. (p. 44)

[105] Cf. Ps. xlviii. (p. 44)

[106] Ps. iv. (p. 45)

[107] Ps. iv (p. 45)

[108] Āsi. The aorist tense is applicable to first, second, or third person singular, and 'myself' is not in the Pali. Hence the former half of the verse might have been said equally to or by the Therī. (p. 45)

[109] I.e., ignorance (Commentary). (p. 45)

[110] Sītibhūt' amhi nibbutā, lit., 'Become cool am I, content,' or 'at peace.' See Introduction. The phrase is an oft-recurring refrain, implying–whatever other implications of peace, happiness, serenity went with it–the attainment of Nibbana. 'Rapt and intent' (samādhinā) is the Commentary's explanation of 'disciplined thought.' (p. 45)

[111] Contained in Saŋyūtta Nikāya, i. 68-70; see also 97, and Rhys Davids, Buddhist India, 10, on the affection of brother and sister for their grandparent. The 'young creatures' in the parable are a prince, a serpent, a fire, and a bhikkhu. All four are great potential agencies for good or evil. Pronounce Pase'nădĭ. (p. 46)

[112] See p. 15, n. 1. (p. 46)

[113] See p. 15, n. 1. (p. 47)

[114] See p. 15, n. 1. (p. 47)

[115] Presumably Ps. vii. (p. 47)

[116] Or tee, surmounting the cupola. Vipassi was the first of the seven Buddhas of the Pitakas. (p. 48)

[117] read vāreyyadivase (cf. p. 276, verse 464), which makes sense anyway. It would appear that Carabhūta (pronounced Chără-) would have been the object of her choice. (p. 48)

[118] Animittaŋ, ideals not depending on what is impermanent, or on what makes for sorrow, or on the presence of a persisting soul-entity (Rhys Davids, Yogāvacara's Manual, xxvii., xxviii.). (p. 49)

[119] Māna, conceit, pride, vanity, one of the seven forms of bias. Majjh. Nik., i. 109, 110; Vibh., 340. Translator's Buddh. Psy., 298, n. 3. (p. 49)

[120] Cf. Rhys Davids, Buddhist India, 25, 40. (p. 49)

[121] The Bojjhangas or Sambojjhangas; lit., parts or limbs of Bodhi. They were mindfulness, research in the Dhamma, energy, joy, serenity, concentration, equanimity (B. Psy., 84, n. 2. Cf. Ps. xxxi.). (p. 49)

[122] 'For inasmuch as the Exalted One is the very Body of the Norm, to discern the Ariyan Dhamma which is His is to see Him. The Buddhas and other Ariyans are said to be seen, not only by the sight of their visible shape, but also by insight into the Ariyan Dhamma, according as He said: "Verily, Vakkhali, he that seeth the Norm, he seeth me"' (Saŋyutta Nikāya, iii., p. 120). '"The Ariyan disciple who hears, brethren, is one who sees the Ariyans"' (Commentary). (p. 49)

[123] This is the Elder Sumangala, who in his verse (Theragāthā, 43) celebrates his release from three 'crooked things' (supra, Ps. xi.)–rom sickle, plough, and spade. (p. 50)

[124] Expressed in the text by the representative drudgery of the 'mortar' (musala). (p. 50)

[125] In the Pali the first two lines depart from the śloka metre, being apparently a curious variety of some metre I cannot identify. See Introduction. The last two lines revert to the śloka, sukhato being an obvious gloss. Quite literally, the quaint and elliptical passage runs: 'The shameless one me "sunshade" only,' which the Commentary explains as 'My husband calls me not even an umbrella which he makes for his livelihood.' There seems nothing in verses or Commentary to justify Dr. Neumann's inference that her husband lived on her adulterous earnings. Toil has spoilt her looks, and he takes no further pleasure in them. (p. 50)

[126] Cf. Ps. lxvi. (p. 50)

[127] Vinaya Texts (S.B.E. xx.), iii., p. 360. (Pronounced 'Chul'la.') Benares was the capital of Kāsī. On the name Aḍḍha Kāsī (lit., half-Kāsī), see op. cit., ii. 195, n. 2. (p. 50)

[128] Tisso vijjā. The Brahmanic phrase, tevijjo, often recurring below – e.g., Ps. xxxvii.–and signifying 'versed in the three Vedas,' was, according to Anguttara-Nikāya, i. 163-5, adopted by the Buddha and applied to the three attainments of paññā, entitled reminiscence of former births, the Heavenly Eye, and the destruction of the Asavas. (p. 51)

[129] I.e., before this present age. (p. 51)

[130] Cf. Ps. iii. (p. 51)

[131] One of the (later elaborated) twenty-four Buddhas. (p. 52)

[132] Rājgir (the ancient burg) is surrounded by some seven hills. See Cunningham's Archæological Survey, iii., Pl. xli. (p. 52)

[133] Lit., 'Now is my heart (or mind) set free!' For lovers of the mountain, the 'great air' and the sense of spiritual freedom will be tightly bound up. The age of the two climbers throws into relief the arduousness of their spiritual ascent. (p. 52)

[134] Mettā in the Commentary. Mittā=amica. Cf. Ps. viii. Both Mittā and Mettikā (Ps. xxiv.) may be patronymics, derived ultimately from Mitra (Mithra), the Vedic propitious, friendly Day or Sun god. (p. 53)

[135] In the Apadāna it is 'a religieux' of no specified Order. (p. 53)

[136] See Rhys Davids, Buddhism, 139-141. (p. 53)

[137] One of the twenty-four. (p. 54)

[138] I.e., she of the Lotus (p. 54)

[139] Abhaya's verses (Th., 26, 98) do not refer to his mother. (p. 54)

[140] Fearless. (p. 55)

[141] Second of the Seven Buddhas. (p. 55)

[142] B. Psy., p. 69. The 'foul things' were corpses or human bones, such as might be seen in any charnel field, where the dead were exposed and not cremated. I have before me a photograph of a Ceylonese bhikkhu seated in the cleft of a rock contemplating two skulls and other bones lying before him–a modern snapshot of a scene that might be 2,500 years old instead of 250 days. (p. 55)

[143] Lit. (as in many other verses), 'done is the will, or rather the system or teaching (sāsanaŋ) of the Buddha.' Verses 36, 38, and 41 (except the last two lines) are in the text identical, though varied in translation. (p. 55)

[144] Cf. 2 Cor. x. 5 (p. 56)

---

[145] Cf. Ps. iii. and xxiii. (p. 57)

[146] Salaḷa-pupphāni, possibly shoots of the Indian pine (sarala). (p. 57)

[147] The Commentary holds that, by 'word' or teaching (sāsana) here were meant passages of doctrine declaring how rare was the opportunity, and brief, of birth as a human, when Nibbana might be won, illustrated by similes like that of the blind tortoise (Majjh., iii. 169; infra, 500) (p. 57)

[148] See below, xlvii., li. (p. 58)

[149] Lit., the Khandhas, the nature of sense-perception and the elements of my being. Cf. Ps. xxxviii. for a more literal translation. (p. 58)

[150] See Ps. xx. (p. 59)

[151] 'Void,, i.e., I am empty of greed, ill-will, and dulness, the three springs of all evil. 'Signless,' i.e., I am free from all attachment to anything 'marked' as impermanent, evil, or having a soul. See Ps. xix., ver. 20, n. 1. (p. 59)

[152] See Pss. iii., xxiii. (p. 60)

[153] Nāga, a more poetic term for elephant. (p. 60)

[154] Dantikā=little tamed (woman). (p. 60)

[155] The King contemporary with Gotama Buddha was Pasenădĭ. (p. 61)

[156] Meaning Psyche, or, more literally, 'alive,' 'Viva.' (p. 61)

[157] A staple figure used when any great number is meant. Of course, the circumstances of infinitely numerous previous lives of Ubbirī are here implied. (p. 61)

[158] She not only reaches it as a lay-woman, but her subsequent entry into the Order is not even mentioned. (p. 62)

[159] A free rendering of the one word parinibbutā. Cf. ver. 132. (p. 62)

[160] The orthodox sequence is Norm, Order, here inverted metri causâ. The inversion is actually met with in later Buddhism. (p. 62)

[161] Here it is not stated in which Buddha's ministry this took place. (p. 62)

[162] In earliest times simply the hut or chalet, in a cluster of such, reserved for the Buddha or leading teacher, consisting of open hall and sleeping chamber adjoining. (p. 62)

[163] The term of human life was believed to have been much longer in earlier ages. See Dīgha Nikāya, ii., p. 3. Cf. Gen. v. (p. 62)

[164] See p. 1. (p. 62)

[165] See Ps. xii. (p. 62)

[166] The word for spirit, -devatā, lit. deity, is feminine, as are all abstract nouns in -tā; but whether tree-spirits were more usually conceived of a male or female, or as sexless, is not clear. Cf. the plates in Cunningham's Bharhut, and, on tree-spirits generally, chaps. ii. and iii. in Mrs. Philpot's The Sacred Tree. See also Appendix. (p. 63)

[167] Sukkā. (p. 63)

[168] Under which Buddha is not stated. (p. 64)

[169] Kiŋ-kusalaŋ-gavesinī. Cf. D., ii. 151: Kiŋ-kusalānvesī. (p. 64)

[170] Members of religious orders frequented 'parks' (ārāmā) or 'pleasaunces' when dwelling near towns. (p. 64)

[171] Every Buddha had his specific kind of Bo-tree under which he attained Buddhahood (Dīgha N., ii., p. 4). (p. 64)

[172] Let it be noted that the heroine is an Indian widow! (p. 64)

[173] Meaning 'Alpina' (selo=rock, or crag). (p. 65)

[174] In the Bhikkhunī-Saŋyutta (translated in the Appendix) she is so called. Āḷavī is stated to have been thirty yojanas (c. 260 miles) from Sāvatthī and twelve from Benares (Spence Hardy, Manual of Budhism, 262; Legge's Fa Hien, chap. xxxiv.; Yuan Chwang (Watters), ii. 61). The conversion of King Āḷavaka is deseribed in Sutta Nipāta, pp. 31. ff. (S.B.E., x. 29-31), and Saŋ. Nik., i. 213-215. (p. 65)

[175] Sankhārā, i.e., their potency to lead to rebirth. (p. 65)

[176] Cf. the reply of Āḷavīkā in Appendix, commencing with a direct contradiction omitted in this psalm. (p. 65)

[177] Cf. her verses in Appendix. (p. 66)

[178] Second of the Seven (Pitaka) Buddhas, son of King Aruṇa (sic in Dīgha N., ii. 7) and Pabhāvatī. (p. 66)

[179] Ps. xxvii. (p. 66)

[180] Cf. Ps. lii. (p. 66)

[181] The daughter of a Neapolitan told me that the identical idiom exists in Italian: Una mente lunga di due dità. (p. 66)

[182] It is regrettable that, in this work, Somā's dignified retort lacks the noteworthy extension given to it in the Saŋyutta version (see Appendix):

'To one for whom the question doth arise:
Am I a woman in these matters or

Am I a man? or what not am I, then?–
To such a one is Māra fit to talk!' (p. 67)

183 Dr. Neumann translates Kapilāni by 'the Blonde' (kapilo is auburn, reddish), as if in keeping with the soubriquet of the other Bhaddā (Ps. xlvi.). I have not done so because elsewhere a soubriquet is always explicitly accounted for in the Commentary, and here nothing is said. Moreover, and this is fairly conclusive, the Apadāna chronicle, quoted in the Commentary, makes Bhaddā 'daughter of Kapilā the twice-born (brahmin).' Kapilānī, therefore, refers to her family. and should be Kāpilānī. The Phayre and Paris MSS. of the Therīgāthā both read Kāpilāni, so does Vin., iv., 290, 292. (p. 68)

184 On the three Sāgalas, see Rhys Davids, Buddhist India, p. 38. According to the Apadāna this was the capital of the Maddas (cf. Ps. lii.). Mahātittha, the 'great ford,' was a brahmin village in Magadha. (p. 69)

185 Titthiyārāma, near the Jeta Grove at Sāvatthi. (p. 69)

186 Defined in the Pitakas as meaning Buddhas, Silent Buddhas, and their disciples. This judgment is the subject of Ang. Nik., i. 23-26. (p. 69)

187 Mahā-Kassapa became the leader of the Buddhist Order when the Buddha had passed away. According to the Apadāna, Kassapa was identical with Pippali, her husband, and had been her husband in three former lives. Kassapa was either the family name or the personal name; Pippali either the personal or the local name. See Dialogues, i. 193. His story is fully told in the Commentary on the Psalms of the Brothers, and in that on Ang. Nik., i. 23. (p. 69)

188 The metaphor is not Buddhist. The Pali reads 'by these three wisdoms' (etāhi tīhi vijjāhi). See Ps. xxii. 26. The case of Bhaddā is noteworthy as being the only one where wife and husband–united for so many ages–act in harmony up to the day when, having aided each other in donning the religious dress, they leave the world together,

then part on their several ways to the Buddha, enjoying thereafter good comradeship in the Order. So she in the Apadāna:
'Thereafter soon I won the rank of Arahant.
Ah! well for me who held the friendship wise and good
Of glorious Kassapa.' (p. 69)

[189] Chaḷabhiññā. Abhiññā in the previous Psalm is rendered 'mystic lore profound.' The Six, otherwise defined as paññā (Dialogues of the Buddha, i., p. 57) and as vijjā (ibid., p. 124), are Iddhi, the Purified Hearing, knowledge of the thoughts of others, memory of former lives, the evolution of the lives of other beings, the extinction of the Āsavas (see Vibhanga, 334). The last was virtually identical with Arahantship. (p. 71)

[190] Lit. only, 'soaked with the passion of sense desires,' and explained as one whose mind was wetted by an exceedingly strong inclination, by an abundance of passionate desire for all the pleasures attainable through the senses. The metaphor of 'soaking' (avassutā) is nearly akin to that in the cardinal defects called Āsavas, one of which is precisely the predilection described above, and the extinction of which are named as the sixth abhiññā in the following verses. (p. 71)

[191] The last five words are only implicit in the Pali. Cf. Ps. xxx. 43. Compare Dhammadinnā's help with that given by Paṭācārā, Ps. xxx. (p. 72)

[192] See Dialogues of the Buddha, i., p. 89. (p. 72)

[193] With Sāriputta and Mahā-Kassapa he belonged to the greatest of the Buddha's apostles. (p. 72)

[194] Theragāthā, verses 1150-57. (p. 72)

[195] There is no change in the Pali metre of this Psalm, but seventeen years ago the subject tripped off of itself into the metre as above, and I have so left it. (p. 72)

[196] On 'Second Jhana,' see B. Psy., pp. 43-46. (p. 73)

[197] On Sīha, General of the Licchavis, see Rhys Davids and Oldenberg, Vinaya Texts (S.B.E.), ii. 108 ff. 'Sīha'=lion. (p. 73)

[198] Ayoniso-manasikārā, lit., 'from not attending to cause or source.' (p. 74)

[199] I.e., by continuing my round of rebirths. Cf. the Western idea of suicide–to 'put an end to it all'–with this of 'starting it again.' (p. 74)

[200] Sundarī-Nandā = 'beautiful delight.' (p. 75)

[201] I.e., half-brother. Cf. p. 6. (p. 75)

[202] Aggapuggalo. (p. 75)

[203] See Ps. xix. (p. 75)

[204] An elaboration of two Pali words difficult to render adequately with brevity–ekaggaŋ susamāhitaŋ. (p. 75)

[205] The curious inflexion dakkhisaŋ, the reading adopted by the editors of both text and Commentary, is an aorist (first person singular) termination on the future stem of 'to see.' Dr. Neumann, disregarding the Commentary, takes it as aorist, making Nandā speak all the lines to and of herself. The Commentary divides the speech as above, paraphrasing by passissaŋ an artificially regular future of passati, to see, and a verbal noun, 'one who will see,' like passaŋ, 'one who sees.' In the corresponding Apadāna lines the Mandalay MSS. read the regular future (second person singular), dakkhasi, 'thou wilt see.' Either we must, with the Commentary, read some future form of the verb, or make Nandā repeat herself in verses 84 and 85, instead of responding in 85 to the Master's exordium in 84. Professor R. Otto Franke, in a learned note, most kindly responding to my question, 'does not venture to decide' whether to keep dakkhisaŋ, or adopt one of the other readings. The severe absence of redundancy in these

short poems decides me to follow the tradition, and reserve 'I have seen' for 85: yathābhūttaŋ ayaŋ kāyo diṭṭho. (p. 76)

206 Verse 150 (p. 76)

207 On this interesting place, see J.P.T.S., 1909, art. by Dr. Watanabe. (p. 77)

208 Lit., the Unbound or Free Brethren–i.e., the Jains. (p. 77)

209 See Ps. xlvi. The autobiographical evolution hinted at in verse 89 of the Psalm fits ill with the career sketched in the Commentarial tradition. (p. 77)

210 In the Commentary she is called Mittãkãlikã (a diminutive form). (p. 78)

211 See Ps. xlii., n. 1. (p. 78)

212 Dīgha Nik., ii., pp. 290 ff. (p. 78)

213 Yoniso uppajjantī, a most unusual phrase for mental growth. (p. 78)

214 A phrase from the Commentary. (p. 78)

215 Called Sakulā in the Anguttara (i. 25), but Pakulā in Commentary and Appendix. (p. 79)

216 Paribbājakā. Cf. Rhys Davids, Buddhist India, p. 141. (p. 79)

217 In Pali, simply 'Āsave.' (p. 80)

218 The powers here briefly indicated are the culminating stages of Vijjā or Paññā. See Dialogues of the Buddha, i., p. 124 (§§ 14-16), and passim, and Cf. Ps. xxxviii. (p. 80)

[219] Parato disvā, lit., having seen as Other–i.e., says the Commentary, following the Pitakas (e.g., Majjh. Nik., i. 500), as without Soul or Ego The oldest books specify compounds of act, word, and thought as sankhāra's. (p. 80)

[220] For an uncondensed account from the Manoratanapūraṇī, see Mrs. Bode, op. cit., pp. 768 f. (p. 80)

[221] See Ps. lxiii. (p. 81)

[222] See Pss. xxx., xxxviii. (p. 81)

[223] See Ps. iv. (p. 81)

[224] See Ps. xxxi. 46. (p. 82)

[225] Anantarā-vimokhā 'sim. (p. 82)

[226] Lit., 'I am without longing, born of a stable base.' Possibly the passage, of which there are many corrupt variants, may have been āṇejj' amhi, 'I am immovable.' (p. 82)

[227] Spelt -kesī at the allusion to her in Ps. xlii. For an uncondensed version of the chronicle, see Mrs. Bode, op. cit., pp. 777 f. (p. 82)

[228] See Ps. xii.; Commentary, n. 1. (p. 82)

[229] The average span of life in Kassapa Buddha's era (Dīgha N., ii.). (p. 82)

[230] See Ps. xxxvii. (p. 82)

[231] See Ps. xlii. (p. 83)

[232] The title reserved for the Apostle Sāriputta. (p. 84)

[233] 'Ekaŋ nāma kiŋ? or more fully, 'What is that which is called (named) "one"?' Tho Jains do not appear to have been any more monistically or pantheistically inclined than the Buddhists, hence possibly her lack of ready reply. The systems she is said to have acquired cannot well have included the more esoteric and more jealously reserved Brahmanic lore. It is difficult otherwise to imagine her at such a loss, unless it was because of the extreme vagueness of the question. 'In the beginning there was One only.' . . . 'He is one, he becomes three . . . five,' etc. 'All things become one in prājñā,' and so on:–the oldest Upanishads give plenty of such answers. Conceivably she may have known this monism, but have seen no end or point in it, because, as a sincere Jain, she rejected it. Neither would the Apostle have wished for a Brahmanic reply, except as an occasion to be improved upon. He would be more interested in the analysis and classification of phenomena bearing on the ethical life. Thus, in the ancient catechism, the Khuddakapātha, the question actually occurs: Ekaŋ nāma kiŋ? But the answer is, 'All beings are sustained by food.' Hence 'the point' really was, State any one fact true for the whole of any one class of things. (Cf. Ang. Nik., v. 50, 55.) (p. 84)

[234] Dhammapada, ver. 101. (p. 85)

[235] Lit., having one garment or cloak. The Nigaṇṭhas were ascetics (Dialogues of the Buddha, i. 220, 221). (p. 85)

[236] It is not impossible that Sāvatthi had its Vulture's Peak (Gijjhakūṭa) as well as Rājagaha in Magadha; but the latter peak is the one usually mentioned, and it seems more probable that Curlyhair's legend has been (badly) fitted on to another Bhaddā's Psalm. Cf. Ps. xlii., also Ps. xlvii., lxiii. The commentator is silent on the point. (p. 86)

[237] Great importance came to be attached to a case of ordination–in the case, at least, of a woman–by the Master direct, as was this. Dhammapāla ends his Commentary with a note upon it. (p. 86)

[238] That, from an Eastern standpoint, she incurred no debt as the people's pensioner, but more than repaid their charity by giving them

opportunities for storing merit, is well shown in the following lines. (p. 86)

[239] Thus, as sister of Bhaddā Curlylocks, or, rather, of the immediate personal antecedent of Bhaddā, and of five other eminent women. Sec Ps. xii., n.; and cf. Mrs. Bode, op. cit., pp. 556 f.; and Jātaka 4, Buddhist Birth Stories, pp. 158 f. (p. 86)

[240] When the pains of childbirth set in. (p. 87)

[241] Paṭā, cloak; ācarā, walker (fem.). (p. 88)

[242] Sati is memory plus consciousness, in a reasonable being, of what one is now doing. 'Thy reason' would be more idiomatic English. 'Sister' here (bhagini, not Bhikkhunī or Theri) is the term for the blood-tie, or a term of respect. (p. 89)

[243] The first of the four paths of salvation, Arahantship being the fourth. (p. 90)

[244] Udayabbayo, rise-fall or coming-going. I have merely varied the phrase from line 2. (p. 90)

[245] Lit., 'There was emancipation of the heart' (or mind). It is not easy to avoid jejuneness in rendering faithfully the austere simplicity of this little poem, wherein the terms and metaphors are not rich in import to us as they would be to an early Buddhist. (p. 91)

[246] Cf. with the following, Ps. lviii. (p. 91)

[247] One note in the individual chord sounded in this Psalm and the next is certainly the emphasis laid on the loyalty of the Sisters to their present Mistress rather than to the absent and less directly guiding Master. (p. 92)

[248] On this mythical illness, see Hardy, Eastern Monachism, 85 n. (p. 93)

[249] Bhikkhunī. The charm of the poem lies in the poor woman, an involuntary beggar 'in the world,' 'coming forth,' a voluntary beggar, into the higher Mendicancy, and from the dregs of living, reckoned by worldly standards, setting herself to win the cream of the life of Mind. (p. 93)

[250] Lit., the thing of supreme import or advantage–paramatthe. (p. 93)

[251] Pañcasatā Paṭācārā. Dr. Neumann, who disregards the Commentary throughout as a mere exegesis and of less than no historical value, renders pañcasatā by 'of fivefold subtlety'–die fünfmal Feine–satā being taken as 'one who has sati' (memory, mindfulness, discernment), Sanskrit smṛtā. I believe the expression pañcasatā occurs nowhere else; nor is there anything in the gāthā's to justify the soubriquet. Nor am I concerned to euhemerize the, to us, mythical absurdity of 500 bereaved mothers all finding their way to one woman, illustrious teacher and herself bereaved mother though she might be. Five hundred, and one or two more such 'round numbers,' are, in Pali, tantamount simply to our 'dozens of them,' 'an hundred-fold,' and the like. But, besides this, the phenomena of huge cities and swarming population are not, in countries of ancient civilization, matters of yesterday's growth, as in our case. (p. 95)

[252] The sharp contrast between this chant of consolation and that which any other religious anthology affords is sufficiently interesting. But if the burden of the chant, in its varied iteration, be imagined, not tripped off on the tongue of a cheerful critic or a disapproving other-believer, but uttered in grave, tender accents, coming from a heart that felt intensely because it had so ached, and from a mind that understood and was therefore serene . . . Even so might Bouguereau's 'Vierge Consolatrice' speak, her great wise eyes looking forth over the anguished bereaved sister flung on her lap, while the dead child lies below at her feet.

/

'Lo! ask thyself again whence came thy son

To bide on earth this little breathing-space?'
To face p. 78. (p. 95)

253 Parinibbuttā, Cf. ver. 53. (p. 96)

254 Cf. p. 40, n 3. (p. 96)

255 See Ps. lxix. (p. 96)

256 Nāga, a term not seldom applied to a great and mysterious personality. I can find no English equivalent. (p. 96)

257 More than once in these verses–never, I believe, in prose–the family name of the Buddha is used by the faithful–e.g., Ps. liv. (p. 97)

258 More than once in these verses–never, I believe, in prose–the family name of the Buddha is used by the faithful–e.g., Ps. liv. (p. 98)

259 First of the seven Buddhas of the Pitakas. See Dialogues of the Buddha, ii. 3. (p. 98)

260 See Ps. xii. (p. 98)

261 Cf. Ps. xxxvii. (p. 98)

262 Presented by Bimbisāra to the Order, six miles from Rājagaha. For a more detailed version of this story (I have slightly condensed a slightly less detailed original), see Mrs. Bode, J.R.A.S., 1893, p. 529. ff. (p. 98)

263 Dhammapada, ver. 347. (p. 99)

264 The Apadāna version in ninety-two verse-couplets is then quoted. Arahantship outside the Order was very rare, though not unknown. (p. 99)

265 In the text the usual śloka metre is employed. (p. 99)

[266] I.e., the Khandhas, or five constituents making up a person under conditions of sense experience. (p. 100)

[267] Nandi, sensuous delight, implying more or less love of all three. (p. 100)

[268] These two lines, which are somewhat turgidly amplified, run in literal terseness thus: 'Ye foolish young ones, who know not things as they really have come to be, [those rites] ye have fancied to be purification' (suddhi). (p. 100)

[269] Purisuttamo, 'supreme among men.' (p. 100)

[270] Nakkhattakīlaŋ, constellation-sports. Cf. verse 143 in the preceding Psalm. (p. 101)

[271] This is another subtle stroke of artistry, to let the visual emphasis in the poem culminate in the intenser metaphor of touch. 'Seeing is believing, but touch is the real thing.' The word is frequently so used in the Pitakas, but without the theosophical mysticism of the Neoplatonic ἁφή. (p. 101)

[272] Saddhamma means good teaching (εὐαγγέλιον), not, of course, God's 'spell.' (p. 102)

[273] See this episode in fuller detail in Mrs. Bode, op. cit., p. 523 ff. The two Commentaries agree in all salient points, ours being less detailed. The above is considerably condensed. The Apadāna devotes 190 verse-couplets to the chronicle of this 'Great' Mother of the Sisters' Order. (p. 103)

[274] In the Apadāna he is called Añjana the Sākiyan. (p. 104)

[275] I.e., should be Emperors, either of worldly dominions or else of the hearts of men. (p. 104)

[276] Buddho=awake. (p. 104)

[277] So K. E. Neumann: Erlöser vielem vielem Volk. (p. 105)

[278] Esā Buddhāna-vandanā. Cf. Savonarola's words: '. . . righteousness of living, which is the grandest homage and truest worship that the creature can render to his Creator' (The Triumph of the Cross). (p. 105)

[279] Attho, good, advantage, profit. (p. 106)

[280] Longing to live again, embodied or disembodied. This and the following three terms are the last five Fetters, 'the sundering of which leads immediately to Arahantship.' See Rhys Davids, American Lectures, 141-152. (p. 106)

[281] = Ps. xxviii. and xxx. (p. 107)

[282] Here is a case where Atthakathā and Gāthā are badly welded, as he who runs may read. The commentator, nothing doubting, identifies the Bhikkhunī as Khemā. (p. 107)

[283] Cf. Ps. xxx., xxxviii. The following 'factors' give twenty-five of the thirty-seven known as the Bodhipakkhiyā Dhammā, omitting the four applications of mindfulness (satipaṭṭhānā), the four stages of potency (iddhipādā), and the four right efforts (sammappadhānāni), but introducing the doctrinal four truths. (p. 107)

[284] = Ps. xlviii. (p. 108)

[285] This question sign is a translator's liberty. The Pali reiterates only the final stage of relief and attainment. (p. 108)

[286] See Ps. xlvii., xlviii. (p. 109)

[287] Lit., consider the sankhāras as other, not as self. (p. 109)

[288] Why 'nineteen' I am unable to explain. They may be bodhipakkhiyā dhammā–e.g., the satipaṭṭhānas, the bojjhangas, and the Path=nineteen factors. (p. 110)

[289] Called also Nāla-village. Sāriputta seems to have continued, at times, to reside there (Saŋy. N., iv. 251), and it was there that he died (ibid., v. 161). (p. 110)

[290] These three Sisters are all included in the Bhikkhunī-Saŋyutta as having been tempted by Māra; but there Cālā's reply is put into Sīsupacālā's mouth, Upacālā's is given to Cālā, and Sīsupacālā's is given to Upacālā. See Appendix. (p. 110)

[291] The five indriyas, replacing, in the higher life, the importance, in worldly things, of the five senses–viz., faith, energy, mindfulness, concentration, and insight. (p. 111)

[292] 'Sectaries' are termed pāsaṇḍā. The Commentary connects the word with pāso, snare, net, but by a false etymology. The origin of the term is obscure. 'Without' (ito bahiddhā)–i.e., not of us. (p. 112)

[293] Cf. Ps. xxiv. (p. 112)

[294] Cf. Pss. xxxv., xxxvi. (p. 112)

[295] Cf. Appendix, where this is spoken to Cālā. (p. 113)

[296] =Ps. xxxv. (p. 113)

[297] Lit., 'cutting (loss) of hand or foot,' referring generally, says the Commentary, to the thirty-two constituents of the body (read kāyākārā for kammakarā). (p. 113)

[298] Here indriya, as something to be restrained, not trained–i.e., developed–refers to the senses of external perception (plus sense-memory). See Ps. lix., 182 n. (p. 115)

[299] Cf. Ps. xxxiv. 55. (p. 115)

[300] The 'higher deities' are the two last in these five Deva worlds which, by the Buddhists, were included with hell, the Peta's or ghosts, animals, men, Asuras, and firmamental spirits, in the 'Kāmaloka of sense-desire,' inferior in space to the Heavens of 'Form' and the 'Formless.' They were the Nimmānarati and Paranimmita-vāsavatti gods. In Ps. lxxiii. (Commentary) I attempt a translation of the last two titles of gods, but they are more translatable in prose than in verse. (p. 115)

[301] 'Think upon' is the translator's interpolation. (p. 116)

[302] Quoted from the Samyutta-Nīkāya, i. 31, 133. (p. 116)

[303] A seaport on the north-west seaboard, the Bharoch of to-day. See Jātaka, iii. 188. (p. 117)

[304] Anubrūhaya=vaḍḍheyyāsi (Commentary). The name Vaḍḍha means grow, increase, develop; often applied to religious culture. (p. 118)

[305] Vanatho. Jungle and vice are equally implied in this word. 'Poison-plants'= simply Āsavā. (p. 118)

[306] Vaḍḍha's gāthā commences with a śloka to the same effect, using the same metaphor. Theragāthā, ver. 335-9. (p. 118)

[307] Dhamma. (p. 121)

[308] 'Goods'–lit., cattle or herds–is pertinent, since she had counted on her child for her improved status, which the absence of 'goods' in her own family had made of no account. (p. 121)

[309] Dhammapada, ver. 47, 287. (p. 121)

[310] Cf. Ps. lxviii., ver. 307. (p. 121)

[311] Cf. Ps. ii. and ff. (p. 121)

[312] Cf. Ps. xlvii. (p. 122)

[313] Sanyutta-Nikāya, i. 87, v. 2, etc. (p. 122)

[314] She here incorporates the story of Paṭācārā (Ps. xlvii.) in her own Psalm, as if more fully to utter, as 'Woman,' the pageant and tragedy of the woeful possibilities inherent in 'woman's lot,' whereof her own case was but a phase. Criticism may discern herein another 'fault' – geologically speaking–in the historical concordance between verses and commentary. Yet here, anyway, is a feature that no poem of purely literary construction would ever have borne. And in æsthetic intensity the poem gains wondrously through this groundwave of deeper tragedy underlying Kisā-gotamī's own sorrow, and through the blended victory in the fine pæan at the end. (p. 122)

[315] The Commentary names dogs, jackals, tigers, panthers, cats, etc., as the scavengers of corpses thus exposed. (p. 123)

[316] This line in Pali is simply amatagāmī, going to the ambrosial, or the not-dead. 'State' is a concession to metrical and grammatical exigencies. 'Gone up on'; lit., practised myself in. Note how verses 216-223 carry out the fourfold 'mark' of verse 215.

The metre in the Pali throughout is not the śloka, and is too irregular to be easily classifiable. Cf. that in lines 2-6 above–
Nibbānaŋ, sacchīkataŋ Dhammādāsaŋ avekkhitaŋ.
Ahaŋ amhi kantasallā ohitabhārā kataŋ me karaṇīyaŋ
with the śloka-metre, beginning of next Psalm:

˘ ˘ ˘ ˘ ˘ ˘ ˘ ˘
˘ ˘
— — — — — — — — — — — —
U b h o m ā t ā c a d h ī t ā c a || m a y a ŋ ā s u ŋ s a p a t t i y o .
/
EXCAVATIONS AT JETA-VANA, NOW SAHĒṬH.

To face p. 110. (p. 123)

[317] Iddhi. (p. 124)

[318] Gabbha, or matrix. So also Ang. Nik. Commentary. But cf. Dr. Neumann's note. And below, verse 257. (p. 124)

[319] Lotus-hued. The lengthy legend, or chain of legends, associating the past lives of this famous Therī with the lotus-flower is fully translated from the Anguttara Commentary in Mrs. Bode's Women Leaders, etc., J.R.A.S., 1893, 540-551. It is only interesting as folk-lore, and not as illustrating any point in her Psalm, hence is here omitted. (p. 124)

[320] Uposathāgāre kālavāro pāpuṇi, a phrase I have not yet met with elsewhere. (p. 124)

[321] See Buddhist Psy., 43, n. 4; 57, n. 2; 58. (p. 124)

[322] The standard description of the modes of Iddhi are given in English in Rhys Davids' Dialogues of the Buddha, i. 277. (p. 125)

[323] See Theragāthā, verses 127, 128. See note below, p. 114. (p. 125)

[324] I have read pabbaji, not pabbajiŋ, following the majority of the MSS. consulted by Pischel, as well as the Commentary. It is less forced to read, in sā, 'she,' and not 'I,' where no other pronoun follows (sā'haŋ). Verse (226) thus becomes the comment of Uppălăvaṇṇā on the mother's distressful utterance. (p. 125)

[325] The Pali metre changes here from the usual śloka to a mixed jagatī and trishsṭubh metre, but changes back again after verse 231. Cf. the other version of this Psalm in the Appendix. e.g.:

˘ ˘ ˘ ˘ ˘ ˘

– – – – – –

S u p u p p h i t a g g a ŋ u p a g a m m a p ā d a p a ŋ || (jagatī)

˘ ˘ ˘ ˘ ˘ ˘

– – – – – – –

e k ā t u v a ŋ t i ṭ ṭ h a s i r u k k h a m ū l e || (trishsṭubh) (p. 126)

[326] Māra was himself an adept at this kind of magic (see Majjh. Nik., i. 332). I follow the Commentary and Dr. Windisch (Māra und Buddha, 139 ff.) in making the Sister speak the verse, her special gift being 'mystic potency,' or Iddhi. (p. 127)

[327] Cf. Ps. xxxv. (p. 127)

[328] The Commentary gives her the latter name, of which the former is the diminutive. Possibly Puṇṇikā may have been used to distinguish her from the Therī Puṇṇā of Ps. iii. It is curious that in the Subha-Sutta of the Majjhima Nikāya, where young brahmins come to the Jeta Grove, Anāthapiṇḍika's gift, to interview the Buddha, a slave-girl Puṇṇikā is alluded to in the conversation. Subha says: 'They [certain brahmin teachers] are not able to read the thoughts of slave-girl Puṇṇikā. How should they be able to know the minds of all recluses?' If this is our Puṇṇikā, she would not yet be a Therī, or she would be referred to as such. (p. 129)

[329] Kilesā. For the ten, see Buddh. Psy., pp. 327, ff. (p. 129)

[330] Majjhima Nikāya, i., Sutta xi. or xii. (p. 129)

[331] Udakasuddhika. Believer in purification through water (as a mystic rite), and not through sacrifice by fire. (p. 129)

[332] The Ac(h)iravatī (now Rapti), a tributary (with the Gogra) of the Ganges, flowing past Sāvatthī. (p. 129)

[333] Not specified in the text. (p. 130)

[334] These four last lines are expansions of four brahminical technical terms, each connoting more than we could express with equal terseness:

Tevijjo vedasampanno sotthiyo c'amhi nhātako.

The brahmin student performed, like a new knight, a bath-rite before returning home from his teacher's house. (p. 131)

[335] See Ps. xxii. 26 n. (p. 131)

[336] See Rhys Davids, Buddhist Suttas (S.B.E., xi.), pp. 30-33. (p. 132)

[337] Used in its first intention, Truth-speaker. On this, and on the metre, see Introduction. The 'rune' is the Impermanence of everything. Cf. Ps lxiii. (p. 133)

[338] Upakūlitā, not yet found elsewhere, may be from the root kūl, to burn. (p. 134)

[339] It is interesting that the Commentary speaks of the goldsmith's work of past ages, as if conscious of living (himself) in a decadent period of such arts. (p. 134)

[340] Kokilā, rendered by lexicons 'Indian cuckoo.' The name seems to point to somewhat similar bird-notes. (p. 134)

[341] Lit., as the weak trumpet-flower (plant), the Commentary adding phalita, broken, or fruit-laden, and so heavily drooping. (p. 135)

[342] Lit., more simply, 'like one little root after another.' (p. 135)

[343] I here follow Dr. Neumann, and not the Commentator. The latter calls nāgabhoga an elephant's trunk; the Pitakas apply the term, it would seem, only as in the text. Cf. Majjhima Nikāya, i. 134. (p. 136)

[344] I.e., Latinized, Flavia. Childers instances a red cow so called, and a constellation. (p. 137)

[345] Note her emphasis on work or action (kamma or karma) to meet her father's–the typically worldly man's–failure to discern the fact and value of any 'work' that had no worldly object. (p. 137)

[346] Unspotted by greed, hate, or dulness; full of the A-sekha's qualities–virtue; contemplation, concentration, insight (Commentary). (p. 138)

[347] This phrase is amplified in Sanyutta Nikāya, i. 5: 'They mourn not over the past, nor hanker after the future. They maintain themselves by the present.' Cf. the same attitude prescribed in the Sermon on the Mount (Matt. vi. 25-34). (p. 139)

[348] I.e., she referred him to the true source of the 'weal' he imputed to her. The rest is borrowed from Ps. lxv. (p. 139)

[349] Cf. Psalm lxv. (p. 140)

[350] Pronounce Chāpā. The name of her native district has, so far, not been met with elsewhere. (p. 140)

[351] An Ājīvaka (-ika), described in Dialogues of the Buddha, i. 221. (p. 140)

[352] I.e., when he left the Bo-tree as Buddha and went to preach his first sermon at Isipatana by Benares. The meeting is told in Majjhima Nikāya, i. 170, 171, and Vinaya Texts, i. 90 (p. 140)

[353] In the Majjhima Nikāya there is another śloka before the last above, in which the Buddha says, 'I am worthy,' etc., thus:
'I am the Arahant [i.e., worthy] of the world, I am
The Guide supreme, the one Truly Awake.
Cool and serene I in Nibbana dwell (nibbuto).' (p. 141)

[354] The 'holy man,' as our tradition might say. He was no Arahant in the Buddhist sense. (p. 141)

[355] Fortunatus. (p. 141)

[356] His humility was due, apart from his natural disposition, to his having no status among a group of independent huntsmen. (p. 141)

[357] This ranked among the five 'topmost' heavens of the 'world of form,' or Brahma-world. See Buddh. Psy., p. 334; Dīgha N., ii. 52. (p. 142)

[358] The Commentator explains this intrusion of Nāla, a village 'in Magadha, near the Bo-tree' (of Gayā) (see Ps. lix.), by saying it was Upaka's native place, and that the pair had gone to live there. As he was the trappers' middleman, and therefore in frequent communication with them, this would locate the Vankahāra country in the forests or jungles immediately to the south of Magadha, Gayā being in South Magadha. (p. 143)

[359] This river flows from the watershed south of the Ganges past Gayā, and the Buddha was coming from it when Upaka first met him. But the Buddha, in the Commentary, is said to have awaited Upaka at Sāvatthī to the north-west. Upaka sets out 'westward' to find him. The geography here forms a pretty crux. Whatever may be decided by archæologists in the near future as to the site of Sāvatthī, that site was north-westward of Gayā. (p. 144)

[360] Keeping the right side toward the object of adoration in walking around him. (p. 144)

[361] See Ps. li. (p. 146)

[362] An idiomatic phrase for a pæan or congratulatory or proclamatory speech. Cf. the two discourses so named, Majjhima N., i., pp. 63. ff. (p. 147)

[363] Vāsiṭṭhī, it will be remembered, is in her legend represented as losing but one child. The Commentary, undaunted by this discrepancy, explains it by the grief-distracted state of the father. Her name is that

of a brahmin gens–the Vāseṭṭhas–yet she is not called a brahmin in her own legend. On the other hand, her individual point of view regarding the Dhamma is very consistently reproduced. Dr. Neumann, ignoring the Commentary as elsewhere, sees in Vāseṭṭhī, or Vāsiṭṭhī, the family name of Sundarī, introducing a very baffling complication into the dramatic simplicity of the Psalm quá ballad. (p. 147)

[364] Nirupadhi–i.e., of how to live so as to undo the conditions or bases for rebirth. The following line reads literally: 'I, being one who had understood the Gospel, dispelled my child-grief then and there.' (p. 148)

[365] Ps. lix. 186. (p. 148)

[366] See Ps. xxii. n. (p. 148)

[367] Lit., I give thee a full bowl. (p. 149)

[368] For this and one half the next verse (327, 328) the Pali verses become redundant. Two are irregular in metre, one has an additional half śloka. No gloss, apparently, has crept into the text. Conceivably the redundancy may be intentionally used to express the abundance of her heritage–that papañca to which the higher life, as a simplification, selection, elimination, stood in sharp contrast. (p. 149)

[369] See verse 349 n. Lit., food left over, scraps. (p. 150)

[370] Tradition places this speech in the mother's mouth. Dr. Neumann's guess ascribes it to the Bhikkhunī who receives Sundarī into the Order. But the whole tone of it, especially the last sentiment–paraloke anāsavā–is that of the laity's point of view. The mere routine to sustain life becomes a tapas to win future compensations. No word is said of the real object of the religious life–the training of the mind and emotions. And salvation here and now—diṭṭhadhamme anāsavā—was the goal of those entering the Order. Cf. Ps. lxx. 349, ff for the Sister's point of view. In this Psalm I follow the Commentary, which does not

interrupt the little drama with its expositions, but gives them separately. (p. 150)

[371] Cf. Ps. xlv. 104. (p. 150)

[372] So Sundarī went with Bhikkhunīs to Sāvatthī, and, entering the Vihāra, saw the Master sitting on the Seat of Doctrine. And, thrilled with a glory of joy and gladness, she said a verse, as if to herself. (p. 150)

[373] It is clear from this affirmation–viz., that she was Anāsavā– that Sundarī was Arahant. Curiously, hers is the sole case where the attainment is not explicitly recorded. She is only said to be tevijjā. To be Anāsavā was the sixth and last stage in vijjā or paññā or abhiññā.

Thus she spoke, declaring her AÑÑĀ, by way of expressing her joy. Then the Master, to relieve her nervousness, asked her: 'But whence comest thou? and wherefore? and who is this Sundarī?' Then she made answer: 'Lo! from Benares. . . .' (p. 151)

[374] Brahmana! Cf. Dhammapada, ch. xxvi; Dialogues of the Buddha, i, 138-140; Neumann, op. cit. 347, n 2. (p. 151)

[375] She had travelled approximately rather under 300 miles for this pilgrimage. But she was near the end of her infinitely long life. (p. 151)

[376] Na bodhāya na santiyā: not for enlightenment, lit., being awake, or peace. George Eliot has lines in sympathy with Subhā:
'Nay, falter not–'tis an assured good
To seek the noblest–'tis your only good,
Now you have seen it; for that higher vision
Poisons all meaner choice for evermore.' (p. 152)

[377] Literally, for samaṇa's or recluses (religieux). (p. 153)

[378] Lit., left over, given as alms. Cf. Jātaka, iv. 380. (p. 153)

[379] Cf. Ps. lxix. 329 n. (p. 153)

[380] I read with the Commentary mahesihi. Cf. the te on next line and 361. (p. 153)

[381] These are similes occurring in discourses ascribed to the Buddha – e.g., Ang. Nik., iv. 128; Saŋy. Nik., v. 112-114; iv. 189, 198; Udāna, 24; Majjh. Nik., i. 130, etc. (p. 154)

[382] Lit., Bringer-along of its (the way's) own affliction. (p. 154)

[383] 'Ujuko nāma so maggo.'
'Straight' is the name that Way is called. (Saŋy. Nik., i. 33.) (p. 155)

[384] Mahesino, as in 350. (p. 155)

[385] See Ps. lxiv. (p. 155)

[386] Bhūtapati; issaro, lord or god of beings in the three planes of sense, says the Commentary; presumably gods, men, and animals. Note that she is not called Queen or Goddess, but pati (masculine). (p. 155)

[387] Jīvakā Komārabhacca, physician to King Bimbisāra at the court of Rājagaha, is a very prominent layman in the first chronicles of the Order, prescribing for its members on different occasions. See Vinaya Texts (S.B.E.), i. 191, ii. 173 ff., iii. 102; Majjh. Nik., i. 368 ff.; Dīgha Nik., i. 49 (Dialogues, i. 67), in which the Grove is mentioned. (p. 157)

[388] The metre now changes from śloka to that termed vetālīya, or, at least, to a metre which in later literature became formulated under that name. It runs approximately thus ('What have I,' etc.):

ᵕ ᵕ ᵕ ᵕ ᵕ ᵕ ᵕ ᵕ ᵕ ᵕ ᵕ ᵕ ᵕ

— — — — — — || — — — — — —

K i n t e a p a r ā d h i t a n m a y ā y a n m a ŋ o v a r i y ā n a t i t t h a s i ?

ᵕ ᵕ ᵕ ᵕ ᵕ ᵕ ᵕ ᵕ ᵕ ᵕ ᵕ

ᵕ ᵕ — — — || — — — — —

Na hi pabbajitāya, āvuso, puriso samphussa nāya kappati. (p. 158)

[389] 'Although,' remarks the Commentator, 'in that wood there was then nothing of the sort. But this he said, wishing to make her afraid.' (p. 159)

[390] Lit., 'Come, dwell in a house.' (p. 160)

[391] The mythical central mountain of the universe, called also Sineru. (p. 161)

[392] Suṇṇa, for the earnest Buddhist, connoting both solitude and the ejection of the Ego-delusion. Cf. Ps. xxxi. 46. (p. 162)

[393] I have filled up the somewhat elliptical style of the text from the Commentary. (p. 162)

[394] Cf. Balzac's philosophe: 'Tiens,' dit-il, en voyant les pleurs de sa femme, 'j'ai décomposé les larmes. Elles contiennent un peu de phosphate, de chaux, de chlorure de sodium, du mucus et de l'eau.' – La Recherche de l'Absolu. (p. 163)

[395] On this curious Psalm see Introduction. (p. 165)

[396] See n. to verse 405. (p. 165)

[397] = Slave of the sage. (p. 165)

[398] Pāṭaliputta. On the rise of this city as the capital of the Mauryan dynasty, and the Buddha's prophecy of that rise, see Rhys Davids, Buddhist Suttas, xi., pp. xv. 18; Buddhist India, pp. 262 ff., where the testimony of Megasthenes is largely quoted. (p. 166)

[399] On Ujjenī and Sāketa, see Rhys Davids, Buddhist India, pp. 39, 40; Neumann, op. cit., 361 n. They may have been some 500 miles apart,

and the journey would be largely by river. Cf. Rhys Davids, op. cit., 103. (p. 166)

[400] The Commentator interprets the Vedic infinitive kātuye, 'do,' as meaning kātu' yye, 'do, lady.' (p. 168)

[401] My reading of this very obscure passage–jināmhase rūpinin Lacchin or rūpinī Lacchī–is suggested by my husband, and differs from that of Dr. Neumann, who has felt compelled to doctor the text. Commentary: 'Defeated by the goddess Sirī (Śrī) clad in human dress'–i.e., Isidāsī, as personating the fickle goddess of chance. Thus they call her 'Luck!' I cannot believe that, had the young divorcee been enceinte, she would have been sent home so ignominiously, or that the tale would have been silent about the child when born. (p. 168)

[402] Vinayadharā, who could repeat the Vinaya-Pitaka. This proficiency was Paṭācārā's to a special degree. See Ps. xlvii.; Ang. Nik., i. 25. (p. 169)

[403] Brahmins. (p. 169)

[404] Nijjaressāmi. This was the ascetic aspect taken of the religious life. As a Jainist opinion, it is criticized by the Buddha in the 'Devadaha Sutta,' Majjhima Nikāya, ii. 214 ff. (p. 169)

[405] Dvipada, lit., 'bipeds,' an epithet of the Buddha I do not find elsewhere. (p. 169)

[406] Buddhist India, p. 40; Neumann, op. cit., 366 n. (p. 170)

[407] To ripen or be cooked is the usual metaphor for a cause working out its effect. Note that 'hell' here (nirăyă) is really purgatory. No form of being, for Buddhism, was eternal. (p. 170)

[408] I have discussed this passage in 'Early Economic Conditions in North India' (J.R.A.S., 1901, 880, n. 1) thus: In the second line, which Dr. Neumann renders 'Vom Tische Reicher lasen wir die Reste auf,' I take

the compound dhanikapurisapātabahulamhi (Commentary: iṇāyikānaŋ purisānaŋ adhipatanabahule bahūhi iṇāyikehi abhibhavitabbe) to mean 'fallen into the power of usurers.' This leads up to the next line, giving a point to it which is lacking in the rendering alluded to.

I am unable to classify the metre throughout this poem, from the first line:
nagaramhi kusumanāme Pāṭaliputtamhi pathaviyā
to the last:
dāsī va upaṭṭhahantiŋ tassa pi anto kato mayā (p. 170)

409 See Ps. lxi., n. (p. 172)

410 The two Kings and their capitals are all names unknown in Indian records. Vāraṇavatī=having elephants, or ramparts. Koñca = heron. (p. 172)

411 Cf. Ps xli. In the Commentary, p. 273, read, for patikulamanasikāraŋ, paṭikkūla°. (p. 173)

412 Sāsanakārā=, according to the Commentary, Ariyans–i.e., Arahants, including the Buddhas. Just below, sāsana is rendered by 'system.' Sumedhā=very wise. (p. 173)

413 See note, verse 436. (p. 174)

414 In Pali 'no eternal rebirth.' (p. 174)

415 Rebirth in 'hell,' as animal, as 'ghost,' as demon, are the four ('purgatorial lives,' vinipāta, in 452); as human or as god. the two. (p. 174)

416 The Ten Powers peculiar to a Tathāgata are: (1) He knows thoroughly right and wrong occasions; (2) he knows thoroughly the effect of all karma-series; (3) the methods for accomplishing anything; (4) the elements (data) of the world; (5) the various tendencies,

inclinations, of beings; (6) the capacities of beings; (7) the nature and procedure of all contemplative disciplines; (8) former lives; (9) he has the 'celestial vision'; (10) he has realized the intellectual emancipation of the Arahant (A., v. 33 ff.). (p. 174)

[417] Kāyakalinā asārena. The rendering of the former obscure term is, perhaps, a trifle forced, but was chosen from the use of kali in Jātaka, v. 134 (=khela, spittle, froth), because of the juxtaposition of asāra=pithless, without essence (cf. Saŋy. Nik., iii. 140), in preference to the more usual association of kali with gambling. See ver. 501. (p. 174)

[418] Vāreyyam. So above, lit., 'Let there be choosing for thee, child,' the term for marriage in high life, whether or no the woman had any voice in the matter. (p. 175)

[419] Lit., 'What is it like?' (p. 175)

[420] Apetaviññāṇo. (p. 175)

[421] Yoniso aruciŋ. Cf. Pss. xxx., xxxviii., lvii. (p. 176)

[422] Cf. Samyutta Nikāya, iii. 149: 'Eternal, brethren, is the wandering (saŋsāro)–nor is the beginning thereof revealed–of them, who, hindered by ignorance and fettered by craving, run to and fro, and wander (among rebirths). . . .' So op. cit., v. 431: 'It is because we had not grasped the Four Truths, brethren, that we have run and wandered up and down so long, both I and you.' (p. 176)

[423] 'In the Nirayas.' See p. 162, n. 1. (p. 176)

[424] The Commentary holds she went on to the other 'signs'–Ill, or Sorrow, and Soullessness. (p. 177)

[425] A mythical ancestor of Sumedhā's and the Buddha's people, the Sākiyas. Mentioned in Ang. Nik., ii. 7; Jātaka, ii. 310, iii. 454 ff.;

Dīpavansa, iii. 5; Mahāvansa, 8, 231; Milindapañha, 115, 291, etc. (p. 177)

426 These similes are all quoted from Majjhima Nikāya, i. 130, 364 ff. Cf. Saŋy. Nik., i. 128; Ang. Nik., iii. 97. See below. (p. 178)

427 The text in these four lines gives merely the metaphor As this would call up no associated similes in us, I expand the terms after the similes in Majjhima Nikāya, 54th Sutta, whence they are borrowed. (p. 178)

428 A simile frequent in the Nikāyas. Presumably muslin turbans, let alone oily hair-dressing, often caused such mishaps. Cf. Saŋy. Nik., i. 108, v. 440; Any. Nik., ii. 93, etc. (p. 178)

429 These and the following verses are apparently allusions to the first Vagga of the Anamatagga Saŋyutta ('World-without-end' Collocation) in the Saŋyutta Nikāya, vol. ii., 178 ff. The only feature lacking there is the perennial blood-flow–a point not without interest in the history of the Pali Canon. The bone-cairn gāthā in the Vagga is quoted by the Commentator, and runs thus:

'But one man's bones who has one æon lived
Might form a cairn–so said the Mighty Seer–
High as Vipulla, higher than the Peak
Of Vultures, mountain-burg of Magadha'–

i.e., the ancient hill fortress of the Magadhese before they built their capital Rājagaha in the plain. No more ancient remains than these in India have yet been identified (Rhys Davids, Buddhist India, 37).

The repetition in verses 496, 497 is curious in a work where redundancy is so severely repressed. Either it goes to strengthen the symptoms that the last two Psalms are by a different and later hand, or else two versions have here been incorporated. In 496 Sumedhā first speaks to all her three chief hearers: 'Call ye to mind' (saratha); the following admonitions are to the Prince only: 'bear in mind' and 'remember' (sarāhi, sara). (p. 179)

[430] In the Vagga just alluded to, the earth itself, and not India (Jambudīpa), is the insufficient source. The 'squares of straw' is from the same Vagga. (p. 179)

[431] This simile is from Majjhima Nik., iii. 169, and Saŋyutta Nik., v. 455. The 'body-parable' is from the latter work (iii. 140). The body (rūpa) is as empty of essence (soul) as the clot of foam drifting down the Ganges. (p. 179)

[432] The danger from crocodiles is, in two of the Nikāyas, used metaphorically for gluttony, one of the four perils of 'those who go down to the water'; it is in the Canon applied only to a Bhikkhu's temptations (Majjh. Nik., i. 460; Ang. Nik., ii. 124). (p. 180)

[433] Nectar=amataŋ, rendered elsewhere in this work by 'ambrosia,' its etymological equivalent. Usually considered one of the many terms for Nibbana, it is here by the commentarial tradition associated with the Dhamma–'the Amata of the Norm brought to us by the Very Buddha in his great compassion.' (p. 180)

[434] Lit., 'Are bitterer by the fivefold-bitter,' explained by the Commentary as 'by the following after of the yet sharper Ill' (dukkhaŋ). Fivefold, referring to the five senses. (p. 180)

[435] Kuthitā may be from one of three roots: kuth, smell; kuth, distressed; kvath, cook (cf. Müller, Pali Grammar, 41). The first, chosen by Dr. Neumann, seems forced here. The last accords best with the other three metaphors of heating process. (p. 180)

[436] Lit., 'The unhostile being' (locative absolute). The Pali has no metaphor of place whatever (p. 180)

[437] Mokkhamhi vijjamāne, lit., exists. Mokkho, probably substituted metri causa for vimutti, is a relatively late term (p. 180)

[438] These two terms are, in the text, the same as the corresponding pair in the preceding line. (p. 180)

[439] In Majjhima Nik., i. 365, where the torch is said to be borne against the wind, not held too long. (p. 180)

[440] A simile from Saŋyutta Nik., ii. 226,–iv. 158; Jātaka, v. 389; vi. 416, 432, 437. (p. 180)

[441] The dog, according to the Commentary, being unable to get away from them, is killed, and presumably eaten. There is no suggestion to the effect that it was acting as watch-dog, and that the pariahs were thieves, beyond stealing the dog. 'Will they do'=kāhinti; Commentary= karissanti. Pischel pronounced the other reading khāhinti as 'no doubt correct,' because of a passage in Hemacandra's Prakrit Grammar. But Dhammapāla, nearer to the age of the Therigāthā Pali by at least 500 years, seems to me to have the stronger claim, let alone plausibility. (p. 181)

[442] She now, says the Commentary, turns to show forth the excellence of Nibbana. (p. 181)

[443] Asambādhaŋ. The Commentary takes this figuratively: 'from the absence of the crowd of corruptions' (or torments, kilesā.). In view of the cardinal importance in the Vinaya of cultivating solitude (cf. Dhammadinnā in Ps. xii.), because, too, of its being the path of the minority, and because of the Suttanta phrase calling the lay life sambādha, and the religious life abbhokāsa, free as air, I incline to take it literally. (p. 181)

[444] [No footnote matches this number in the original text.] (p. 181)

[445] This narrative repeated in from the Apadāna. (p. 182)

[446] The two friends are said to have been Khemā (Ps. lii.) and Dhanañjānī, a brahminee convert (Saŋ. Nik., i. 160). (p. 182)

[447] For these, see Buddhist Suttas (S.B.E., xi.), pp. 251 ff (p. 182)

[448] Khanti. See Dīgha Nik. ii. 49. (p. 182)

[449] Another reading is, 'Thus telling.' (p. 182)

[450] Lit., 'Who has immeasurable wisdom.' (p. 182)

[451] This line expands the Pali word virajjati, according to the commentary, which supplements 'purified' by 'set free.' On the metre of the whole Psalm, see Introduction. (p. 182)

[452] On these, see my Buddhist Psychology, xx.-xxii. (p. 183)

[453] Cf. Selā's Psalm, xxxv. She was the daughter of the King of Āḷavī. (p. 185)

[454] Pamatto. (p. 185)

[455] See Ps. xxxvi., comparing the vastly more interesting reply given here. (p. 186)

[456] Where dotted lines occur, here and below, the reading is as for Āḷavikā. (p. 186)

[457] Not 'to us,' as in the Psalm. (p. 186)

[458] Cf. Ps. lxiii. In the case of elisions, read as for Somā. (p. 187)

[459] By 'ever'–accantaŋ, lit. exceedingly, endlessly–it is conceivable that she alludes, not to her own too common case, as a mother bereaved of a son, but either to endless past bereavements, or to the fact that, as Arahant, she had cut herself off from age-long possibilities of being often again in similar circumstances. Cf., e.g., Ps. xxxiii. (p. 187)

[460] Āsavas. (p. 187)

[461] Vijayā, to whom Ps lvii. is ascribed, is apparently a different person. (p. 187)

[462] Cf. Khemā's Psalm (lii.) (p. 188)

[463] Five sorts of musical instruments are supposed to be implied in this idiomatic phrase–ātataŋ, vitataŋ, ātata-vitataŋ, ghanaŋ, susiraŋ. (p. 188)

[464] I have ventured to bridge over the hiatus, in what Professor Windisch calls the 'loose construction' of this gāthā, by the insertion of 'from all, from. . . .' For what may have been the original, and is the more logical, ending, see Cālā's verses below. As the gāthā in Pali stands here, it seems to mean: '"I see life steadily, and see it whole." Trouble me not with your foolish little solicitations to sensual joys.' (p. 188)

[465] Where the text differs from that of Psalm lxiv. may be seen by the following:

Therigāthā.	Saŋyutta.
Supupphitaggaŋ upagamma padāpaŋ ekā tuvaŋ tiṭṭhasi rukkhamūle	Supupphitaggaŋ upagamma bhikkhuni ekā tuvaŋ tiṭṭhasi sālamūle
Na cāpi te dutiyo atthi; koci na tvaŋ bāle bhāyasi dhuttakānaŋ.	Na c'atthi te dutiyā vaṇṇadhātu idhāgatā tādisikā bhaveyyuŋ. Bāle na tvaŋ bhāyasi dhuttakānaŋ.

On choice of reading in the preceding line, see the Psalm in question, n. (p. 189)

[466] Pronounced Chālā. Cf. Ps. lix., lx. The latter Psalm–Upacālā's–incorporates most of what is here attributed to her sister. (p. 189)

[467] I.e., in the fact or phenomenon of 'being born over and over again.' (p. 190)

[468] Literally, meaning the punishments of criminals, but standing for the ills of life in general. Cf. Ps. lxx., verse 345; lxxiii., verse 505. (p. 190)

[469] Cf. last note to Vijayā's verses above. (p. 190)

[470] In the Psalms, her Psalm is put into the mouth of her sister, Sīsupacālā. (p. 190)

[471] Padhūpito, in the corresponding Psalm paridīpito. (p. 191)

[472]

Sanyutta.	Therigāthā.
Akampitaŋ acalitaŋ aputthujana-sevitaŋ	Akampitaŋ atuliyaŋ aputhujjana-sevitaŋ
Agati yattha Mārassa tattha me nirato mano.	Buddho dhammaŋ me desesi tattha me nirato mano.

(p. 191)

[473] Lit., Thereto is my heart (or mind) devoted. (p. 191)

[474] In the Psalms she is made to utter her sister Cālā's Psalm. (p. 191)

[475] The Psalm ascribed to Selā (xxxv., p. 144) is, in this Appendix, put into the mouth of Āḷavikā, which, in the Commentary, is Selā's patronymic. (p. 192)

[476] Satto, a concrete living entity, not the abstract idea. (p. 193)

[477] Cf. Ps. xlvi. 111 (p. 194)

www.ingramcontent.com/pod-product-compliance
Lightning Source LLC
Chambersburg PA
CBHW051544010526
44118CB00022B/2575